"Though they don't know it, most people—including most Christians—are imprisoned in a deceptive dream that masquerades as reality. You are likely one of those people, and on some level you probably know this. Though you may believe in Jesus, you sense there's something missing in your life.

"In this well-written, theologically insightful, and compellingly argued book, Heather Rae Hutzel helps readers awaken from their imprisonment to discover the radical, beautiful, challenging, dangerous, Jesus-looking life that God calls and empowers all of us to live. I wish every American Christian would read this book!"

— GREG BOYD, Pastor, Woodland Hills Church; President, ReKnew Ministries, author of *Letters From a Skeptic* and *The Myth of a Christian Nation*

"*ESCAPE* couldn't be a better title. This book will take you on a journey of escaping the predictable American worldview that so many of us unintentionally live, toward an adventure of engaging in the story that God has invited all of us to join. This book will give you fresh eyes to who God is, and will bring the story of God in the Bible to life in an actionable way. It will also uncover hidden themes throughout the story of God that are critical to a bold and world-changing faith. Whether you are new to following Jesus, or whether you are a long-time follower of Jesus, prepare to experience the transformation that only comes through your escape."

— TERRY PHILLIPS, Pastor Crossroads Church Florence Campus

PRAISE FOR *ESCAPE*

"*ESCAPE* is a beautiful reminder that the Christian life is meant to begin living heaven on earth right now! Heather invites us to re-think the story that we are currently living and to break free from watered down Christianity. Read this and hear God's invitation to start living that story full of love and beauty, apply it, and you will be free!"

— BRIAN TOLLE, Pastor & Spiritual Growth Leader Crossroads Church Florence Campus

ESCAPE

ESCAPE

Break Free from Mediocre Christianity
and Embrace the Radical, Set-Apart
Life You were Made for

HEATHER RAE HUTZEL

ESCAPE
Break Free from Mediocre Christianity and Embrace the Radical, Set-Apart Life You were Made for

Printed in the United States of America
ISBN: 978-0-9885036-4-9

Editing by Christine Luken: ChristineLuken.com/wordnerd

Learn more information at:
HeatherRaeHutzel.com

To David, my husband,
While you didn't even realize you were doing it,
thank you for being the person who revealed to me
the true character of God. Thank you for being the
one who inspired my escape.

And to Allie, in memory of your escape,
thank you for letting me be your freedom fighter.

"The time has come," he said. "The kingdom of God has come near. Repent and believe the good news" (Mark 1:15)!

Through these he has given us his very great and precious promises, so that through them you may participate in the divine nature, having escaped the corruption in the world caused by evil desires (2 Peter 1:4).

TABLE OF CONTENTS

Introduction: Anything 1

Part I: Escape (Repent) 11

Chapter 1: Escape   13

Chapter 2: Awaken 25

Chapter 3: Fiction 31

Chapter 4: Truth.................................... 39

Chapter 5: Villain 55

Chapter 6: Edit 67

Chapter 7: Hero 83

Chapter 8: Theme 99

Chapter 9: Old 119

Interlude... 131

<u>Part II: Embrace (Believe)</u> 135

Chapter 10: Radical 137

Chapter 11: Character 153

Chapter 12: Cost 165

Chapter 13: Call 177

Chapter 14: Refine 191

Chapter 15: Unveil 211

Chapter 16: End 227

ACKNOWLEDGEMENTS

A huge thank you to everyone who made this book possible. First, to my husband, David, I wouldn't even be on this journey if it weren't for you. Thank you for your support all along the way and for making it possible for me to quit my job to follow wherever the heck it is the Holy Spirit wants to lead us! Without your trust in me and your faith in God, I wouldn't have been able to dedicate these past two years to writing and publishing this book. Thank you for partnering with me on this journey called life and for making it a story worth sharing. I can't wait to see what He has for us next! I love you.

To my lovely editor, Christine Luken, thank you for the time you poured into this project. I am so delighted with the way you polished this manuscript. Your editing skills, guidance, and input are so appreciated. Thank you for not burying my voice, but instead, giving it a megaphone to be as clear and powerful as possible.

To my family, friends, Beta Readers, Street Team, and everyone else who helped make this book possible, you are all wonderful and so very loved. Each of you played such an important role in the journey of this thing we call a book. What a big journey it is. I could not have done it without you.

And to You. You know who you are. You are the One who authored not just this book but this journey. You hold my life in the palm of Your hands. You direct my steps. You never let me fall. You call me out into uncharted territory, and you give me grace when I hesitate. None of these words would exist without you. I am nothing. You are everything. Thank you for allowing me the joy of serving in Your Kingdom, and thank you for asking me to partner with you in writing Your Story.

Throughout this book, the plus symbol (+) is used to indicate where additional material is available.

For behind the scenes, bonus material, discussion questions, a Bible reading plan, and more, be sure to download the complementary guide, *Plan Your ESCAPE.*

You can download it completely FREE at HeatherRaeHutzel.com/PlanYourEscape

ANYTHING

[en-ee-thing]
noun

1. a thing of any kind:
*"Anything is possible with God, even the
impossible."*

"Anything." Such a simple yet dangerous word.

"I will do anything." It's the simplest and most dangerous prayer I've ever prayed. A prayer that wrecked my life and my heart for God. Four simple words. They changed everything.

I thought I understood the meaning of that word. In my mind, I knew what I was saying when I prayed, "God, I'll do anything... *anything*! I just want my life's work to make an eternal impact for Your Kingdom." But I had no idea what I was saying. I didn't realize what kind of power that word held.

On the day I first spoke those words, for me "anything" meant starting a photography business founded on the principle that we are all made in God's image. It was a photography business that I (emphasis on the "I") dreamed of creating.

Shortly thereafter, that word took on a new definition. It came to mean writing a novel that brought to life the story of God, even though I never even had the slightest desire to write a book.

From there, "anything" took on a broader form: public speaking, blogging, a website, and the dream of another book. In time, that dangerous prayer would require me to quit my job long before my husband, David, and I were financially ready to do so. Then something changed.

Somewhere along the way, I decided to take that sweet, little word and toss it into a box. I began defining its meaning. I had grand dreams of what that word could mean for my future. In my mind, it would bring about a lucrative career in writing and an opportunity to become a renowned speaker. I believed it would fund the dream house my husband and I had conjured up in our naïve, little minds. I imagined it would bring about financial prosperity and a life of ease. It was a word that was supposed to be all-encompassing, non-exclusive, and I forced it to mean, "Only the things I say and choose and dream. Only what I want. Only my 'anything.'"

That's when God decided to teach me a new word—humility. In time, God has broken me. He has reminded me of the commitment I made when I first uttered that simple prayer. God is the God of anything. He will do immeasurably more than all we can ever ask or imagine (Ephesians 3:20). Nothing is impossible for Him. God will do everything if only we are willing to say, "Anything."

At this point in my journey, I now revisit that humble word. A word that now, quite literally, means "anything." Not just the things that sound good to me or aren't too far outside my comfort zone but literally "anything and everything." For I can do all things through Him who gives me strength (Philippians 4:13).

This book is a documentation of that prayer, because when I finally said, "Anything," and meant what I said, God threw open the lid to the box that once contained that powerful word. He removed the boundaries. Unhindered and unbridled, God released His Spirit in that moment and gave me a new word—*escape*.

***

Escape is a word that previously held very little significance for me. I've spent my entire life in America, the freest country on God's green earth. While this word had no meaning in my life, in February of 2014, God managed to use it to capture my attention.

I was sitting in my car at a stoplight outside of work. I was waiting to turn into the parking lot next to my building when I received an interesting message from God. Let me set the stage:

Most days, you and I meander through life without much thought to what we are doing, where we are going, or what we are saying. We rarely notice our obliviousness, except for those days when we arrive safely at our destination and realize we can't recall a single stop sign or turn signal we used to get there.

Our brains are hardwired to choose the path of least resistance, forming ruts and well-worn paths for habits and common tasks. Sometimes, I feel if I listen closely, I can hear the steady droning of the well-oiled machine that is my mind and body.

Our brain's ability to create these familiar paths is the reason why we don't have to remember how to use a fork every time we eat. Ruts are necessary for our existence, but if we're not careful, we can form some pretty damaging ruts that lead us to bad places.

Oftentimes, when our brain is on autopilot, we zone out. We all have those moments of white space in our lives. If you're anything like me, you're probably always trying to fill them. Yet, it is often only in those moments of silence that we are quiet enough to hear the still, small voice of God. I've since learned, God is always speaking, but we are not always listening. On that cold February morning, I must have been listening.

I had one of those frightening moments when I suddenly became aware of what I was thinking, a moment when the static in my brain finally dispersed and a megaphone projected the voices in my head loud and clear. I must have been asking myself a question, some sort of deep, implanted conundrum. At the time, I didn't even realize I had such a thought rolling around in my brain. The only reason I "woke up" to my thoughts was because, out of nowhere, the universe provided an answer. God grabbed me by the shoulders and shook me awake so I could see the flashing neon sign before me. There, on the vehicle in front of me, was a small yet powerful word: escape.

Now, let's be clear. The word "escape" just so happened to be the model of the vehicle at the light in front of me—as in a Ford Escape. Strange, yes, but this is how God often speaks. If we are not paying attention, we will not hear Him. How many times before have I seen a Ford Escape and never once been moved to anything beyond my road rage?

I don't even know what question I was pondering in my bored, little brain at that stoplight in downtown Cincinnati, but I do know one thing. God gave me an answer, more like a command, really. I didn't know what He meant by it in the moment, but in time, I would come to learn its meaning. Escape—a word that once held zero significance for me—had now become one of the defining lyrics of my life.

***

Over the past several years, God has been teaching me this very important truth: we, as human

ɟs, are formed by stories. Specifically, we are
ıed by one of two stories. Our identity is the
product of the story in which we choose to live.
Therefore, if we want to change anything about
ourselves, we have to change our story.

There are two main stories that dominate our
existence. One is true, but the other is a work of
fiction. I refer to these two stories as God's Story
and the Story of the World. This idea is not
something I concocted on my own. The Bible
references these two stories and contrasts them
against one another in a relentless sort of way. In
fact, the entire Bible is a story about the battle
between these two stories. Perhaps you've heard
them referenced in their more familiar terminology:
the Kingdom of God and the Kingdom of the
World.

Here's the problem with the Story of the World:
it is pervasive, and it is deceptive. It's like a prison,
a prison in which we are bound. You and I, we are
prisoners, and there is only one thing worse than
being a prisoner: not realizing that you are
imprisoned.

Like in a story about two diabolically opposed
kingdoms, our reality is this: there is a good King
and a real enemy. This enemy would like nothing
more than to keep you blissfully unaware of your
enslavement. His desire is to keep you locked away
in order to use you and abuse you. His plan is to
completely sterilize you from your true purpose and
the story your life was made to tell.

"Not me," you say. "I'm not imprisoned and enslaved. I'm a Christian. I accepted Jesus as my Savior eight years ago!"

That's great; it really is, but here's what I've found. We can be free and yet not have escaped. Just because Jesus has unlocked our prison cells, doesn't mean we have chosen to open the door and step outside.

Escaping is a process. Like a young Indian girl who has been enslaved in the sex trade industry her entire life, we often don't even recognize our slavery. It's the only thing we have ever known. We may hate our mess, our lives, and our circumstances, but they are also comfortable because they are ours. In our case, the prison that holds us captive is a cell locked from the inside.

Our enslavement is a choice. If we desire our freedom, we have to be ready and willing to escape. Once we make the choice to step outside the four walls of our dark, dank prison, we have to be ready for our entire life to change. Slavery and freedom are utterly opposite. There is nothing similar about the two. When we make the choice to escape, we are, in essence, saying, "I am ready and willing to live a life that is completely antithetical to my old way of life."

What we will see as we journey together is that Jesus came to rescue us from our slavery. In essence, He came and unlocked our prison. He bound up and chained our oppressors. He came and burned the law books by which we were once judged. There are no longer any convictions against us. Our sentence has been revoked, but the door to our prison cell requires two keys. Jesus used His very life to break open the lock on the outside of the door; we have the key to unlock the inside.

Every single day, I become more and more aware of this rampant fictional story and its enslaving grip on my life. Each day I have to make a choice to escape and embrace the freedom that was given to me thousands of years ago. The truth is we are all imprisoned, no matter how free we think we are. This is the problem with the Story of the World. It's fiction; it seems true even though it isn't. We need our eyes to be opened. We need to wake up from this seemingly-real dream. But we can't do it alone. That's why I wrote this book.

The truth is we, as humans, were made for so much more! God designed us for a radical, set-apart life. He created us to live in a story that is so much bigger than us. This story is not something to be anticipated. It's not something for us to dream about someday. God's Story is right here and right now. We simply must choose to live in it.

***

This book is based on a very simple principle, the words of Jesus: "Break free, and embrace a radical, set-apart life!"

"Whoa, whoa," you say. "I don't recall Jesus ever saying that."

Oh, but He did, just not with those exact words. Check out what Jesus said in Mark 1:15.

"The time has come," He said. "The Kingdom of God has come near. Repent and believe the good news!"

Let me play this out for us and add some color to what Jesus was actually saying. Here's how I imagine this conversation taking place:

"The Kingdom of God has come near! The Story of God is being written right now," Jesus would say. "You can live the life you were made for now! God designed you for this story. You were made for it. It's right here waiting for you!"

"What must we do to be a part of this story, Jesus?" His followers would ask. "We want to be a part of this Kingdom. How can we have this amazing life?"

"It's simple," Jesus would say. "Turn away from your old story and your old way of life." With a twinkle in His eye, He'd shout, "Escape! Break free from the Story of the World. Repent. Turn away from it."

"That's it?" His followers would question.

"Not quite," Jesus would say while lowering His voice. "After you escape, you must remain that way; no going back. You are free from your old story and your old way of life." His excitement would build. "Believe that it is true because it is! And yes, live like it is true. Embrace a radical, set-apart life. I tell you the truth: you were made for this story! And this, indeed, is very good news."

This is the gospel. It is the very good news that while we are imprisoned slaves, we can escape because we have a redeemer who has unlocked our prison cell. We were made for something more, and that more is here and now. We just have to embrace this truth. We have to believe that what Jesus said about us is reality. God's Story is that reality. It is our truth, and it is our destiny. We were made for this!

If you change your story, it will transform your life. That, my friend, is the means by which you will join the army of God, the Church, and together we will revolutionize the world!

"Here I am! I stand at the door and knock. If anyone hears my voice and opens the door, I will come in and eat with that person, and they with me" (Revelation 3:20).

Jesus is knocking on the door of our prison cell, begging for us to let Him come in and show us His love. By inviting Him into our prison, we are declaring:

"We are ready! We want to know You, Jesus. We are willing to do anything! We are prepared to open the door, step outside, and follow You wherever You go. Whisk us away, sweet Jesus, we are ready to escape!"+

+ For discussion questions for this chapter, check out page 2 in the complimentary guide *Plan Your ESCAPE*. A plan for reading the Bible as one complete story can also be found beginning on page 53 of the guide. You can download it for FREE at HeatherRaeHutzel.com/PlanYourEscape

PART I

ESCAPE
(REPENT)

CHAPTER 1

ESCAPE

[ih-skeyp]
verb

1. to slip or get away, as from confinement or restraint; to gain or regain liberty:
"How will we escape this prison? Will we ever be truly free?"

Contrary to what many might believe, obtaining our freedom is not a quick process. It is not a one and done sort of thing. Our escape does not happen during a single moment in time; rather, it is a journey. Let me tell you about mine.

My journey began long before I even recognized that I was in need of an escape. You see, I grew up going to church. Some may think this would deliver an advantage when it comes to the spiritual arena, but in many ways, it caused me more trouble than good.

As it turns out, my experience was not uncommon. I grew up going to a church that preached morality as the number one virtue. The picture of God I received was a dichotomy of an angry judge and Santa Claus. If I was "nice," God blessed me. If I was "naughty," punishment and curses would ensue. Yes, I was familiar with Bible stories and facts and figures, but none of it was "real" to me. I paid attention in service and Sunday school because I had to. Secretly, I hated religion. I was a slave to it. I felt bound by the chains of morality. After all, I didn't want to go to hell.

The funny thing is, to the outside world, I appeared to be a spiritual, religious, and faith-filled young adult. I attended youth groups in high school, read my Bible, and prayed (rather, I tried to pray), but something didn't feel right. It all felt forced, like I had to work so hard for it, and yet, God was still glowering down at me with that disappointed glare because I had tried but failed, specifically when it came to prayer. (Why is prayer so difficult?)

Now, I won't say it was all a sham. Looking back, I believe I experienced brief moments, little blips where the clouds parted and the light of God's goodness shone through the window of my prison cell. For the most part, though, I lived a very dark, hollow life.

What amazes me the most? I didn't even understand the very core of the Bible—Jesus. Of all the parts of my story, it always sounds the strangest when I say, "I grew up going to church, but I didn't meet Jesus until I was in my twenties." Yes, I was taught that Jesus was God's Son and that He died for my sins. I was even baptized at age fourteen, but I did it out of a fear of going to hell.

I couldn't understand. Why was God so angry? Why was God so blood-thirsty that His rage had to be taken out on His Son? The only reason I could imagine anyone would "commit" their life to Christ was out of fear that, if they didn't, God would smite them.

Looking back, I doubt I could have articulated any of these thoughts at that point in my life. As a result of my church experience, Jesus became an afterthought. I remember never being super interested in the gospel, the story of Jesus' life, and especially not the story of the cross. It all bored me. I just wanted to know the things I "needed to do" in order to be a "good Christian."

After giving you my backstory, maybe you can understand. Perhaps you can even relate. I'm finding that this "fire and brimstone threat of hell" is pretty pervasive, but it doesn't create true disciples who want to eagerly follow Jesus. It creates terrified servants who do the right thing only because they are afraid of being damned. Instead of producing people who reflect and spread love as Jesus commanded us to do, we are creating robots that spread a spirit of fear. And our preachers are certainly not exempt. For many evangelists, it is their own fear of not "winning souls" that drives them to share the very same fear-inspired message that prompted them to walk an aisle twenty-five years prior. All this does is lead to a spirit of religion, a compulsion to do what is right because you don't want to be wrong.

Now, I'm not saying that we shouldn't teach about hell. Hell is real. I'm not even saying that we should diminish the gravity of the implications of a literal hell. What I'm saying is that there's a real problem when more focus and attention is placed on eternal damnation than on the solution to that damnation—Jesus. The reality of hell is not good news. It is true, yes, but it is not the kind of thing that wins over hearts and souls. Jesus rarely talked about hell during His time on earth. Instead, when He entered a town, His arrival was good news.

A.W. Tozer once said, "What comes into our minds when we think about God is the most important thing about us." He went on to say, "This is true not only of the individual Christian, but of the company of Christians that composes the Church. Always the most revealing thing about the Church is her idea of God."[1] I submit to you this: if the God we follow looks like anything less than Jesus on the cross, then we are not following the real God.

Maybe you too grew up going to church and yet didn't meet Jesus until you were in your twenties, thirties, forties, or fifties. Maybe you grew up going to church and still haven't met Jesus!

---

1. Tozer, A. W. *The Knowledge of the Holy: The Attributes of God, Their Meaning in the Christian Life*. New York: Harper & Row, 1961.

The staggering number of people who live under the banner of this statement floors me, primarily because the Church is supposed to *be* Jesus!

What we need to realize is that we can't know Jesus by just reading a story about Him any more than you could know your spouse or a friend by merely reading a story about them. You have to physically meet the person. You have to experience them. In the case of Jesus, it requires another flesh-wearing, air-breathing human being who is literally acting as His hands and feet before we can see Jesus for who He is. This is who we were created to be, and these kinds of disciples are only created when the Church is following a God that looks like Jesus.

For me, Jesus took the form of my husband, David. David and I met in our high school chemistry class (oh, the irony). We dated our junior and senior years of high school, attended the same college, and were engaged during the first semester of our junior year at university. We then proceeded to wait another two and half years to finish school before tying the knot.

During the months before our wedding, we attended a marriage class, where, for the first time ever, I heard the verse in Ephesians 5 where Paul says, "Husbands are to love their wives as Christ loves the Church" (v. 25). This verse stuck with me, and in the weeks after David and I were married, those words began to resurface.

I seriously have the world's greatest husband (sorry, ladies). It is incredibly apparent to me that he loves me. I have never once doubted his love. I have felt unworthy of it, but never doubted it. So, one day, when good ol' Ephesians 5 flitted through my brain, it suddenly occurred to me, "If this is how David loves me, then how much does Jesus love me?" I broke down. In that moment, Jesus became a real person. I met Him for the very first time. My entire relationship with my husband flashed before my eyes, and I heard Jesus whisper, "All of David's acts of love and kindness and patience... that was Me. Those were all My love letters to you." (Cue the waterworks.)

This was the first of what would become many experiences with Jesus, and it changed everything. EVERYTHING. This was the moment I realized there was a man standing outside my prison door. This was the day I finally heard the incessant yet gentle knocking outside my cell. This was when I realized that Jesus was a real man who loved me and wanted to be with me. Just months later, I would open the door and let Him in.

***

I remember clearly the day I opened the door and let Jesus come inside my prison cell. I was in my car on my way to work, just a few short months after having married the very man who introduced me to Jesus. I was praying. (Praying became easier once I started talking to a real person.) I was having a super intense conversation with Jesus, one that would come to be the most poignant and pivotal discussions we would ever have.

That day, I came to the realization that my life was not making a difference for God's Kingdom. Now that Jesus was real to me, I was ready to be real for Him. I wasn't living a life that was worthy of the unfathomable love I had received. I was experiencing a ridiculous amount of tension. My life looked incredibly ordinary, yet I was made privy to a Jesus who could only be described as someone completely extraordinary.

Something wasn't jiving. So in that moment, I whispered the most dangerous prayer my lips have ever uttered. (Warning: God loves to answer dangerous prayers.) Without even realizing, I reached into the pockets of the dirty, filthy rags that I wore inside my prison cell. Without knowing, I pulled out the key that would unlock the door that enslaved me.

Until that moment, Jesus and I had been talking through a wall, but now we would speak face to face. With trembling hands and much hesitation, I placed the key in the door. The click of the lock mimicked the crack in my voice as I whispered, "Anything."

I felt the door hinge break free. "Anything," I said louder. "I'll do anything!" I threw open the door. "I'll do anything, Jesus. I just want my life's work to make a difference in your Kingdom!"

There are no words to describe the brilliance of His smile. I cannot string together any symbols or analogies that could come close to explaining the feel of His embrace. He swept me up in His arms and spun me around my cell before placing me back on my feet.

"Come!" He said. "Have a seat. We have so much to talk about. It's time to begin planning your escape!"

***

As I said before, obtaining our freedom is not a quick process, though oftentimes we make it sound as though it is. Yes, Jesus died once to cover ALL sin—past, present, and future. Our prison cell has been unlocked by Him, and once redeemed by accepting the grace He extends, we are saved forever, hallelujah, amen. But consider again a young woman bound by the chains of sexual slavery.

If a rescue team is sent in to free the girl, they break down the brothel door, but the girl is the one who has to take hold of her liberator's hand when it's extended. Once she does, she is free, but has she escaped? Just because she is removed from the four oppressive walls that once contained her, it doesn't mean that she has escaped her slavery. She has merely been set free. From there, it is the girl's choice as to whether or not she will continue to live with a slave-like mindset. She will have months, maybe even years, of internal struggle to break the slavery mentality despite being physically free.

You and I, we have a choice. We can be set free here on earth and live unshackled, completely altered lives that only come through escape. Or we can be set free and continue to live with the mindset of a slave, the only difference being the color of the prison walls that enslave us. Then, it will only be through death that we can truly escape.

This is why our addictions, sins, and chains don't completely disappear the moment that we betroth our hearts to Jesus. The reality is we are free. Our shackles have been unlocked, and our prison door is standing wide open. But we continue to loop our chains over our shoulders and trudge around in circles inside our lonely cell. What's worse, often we are encouraged in our performance. Even more terrible than that, sometimes even our churches promote this behavior.

Over the past few years, Jesus has shown me that our escape is a process, a journey, and every journey has a destination. For us, our destination is not someday in the sky, when we die, by and by. That destination is here and now. The Kingdom of God is at hand. The Kingdom of God is here on earth!

On the day I opened my prison door and allowed Jesus to step inside, He took my hand and pulled me out into the sparkling light of day declaring, "Look, Beloved! The time has come. The Kingdom of God is at hand. Repent and believe the good news. It is better than you could have ever imagined!"

Like the young slave girl, the choice is ours as to whether or not we will continue to live as slaves despite our being free. Now, of course our escaping will require some help. We can't do this on our own. We have to have the help of Jesus. This relates back to the story of how I met Jesus through my husband, David.

In order for us to escape, someone has to be Jesus to us, and once we ourselves escape, we must be Jesus to others. We don't have to reach our destination before we can help them. We just need to be slightly further along in the tunnel we are digging, so we can reach back and help pull another forward. On New Year's Eve 2014, I had an experience that painted this picture so perfectly for me.

Just before midnight on New Year's Eve, I fell asleep on our couch. Around 2 AM, I finally woke up and crawled into bed. Of course I couldn't fall back to sleep, so I decided to practice my theme for the year.

In the past, I have chosen one-word themes to mark the beginning of a new year, rather than making resolutions. This year, I did something different. I chose a Bible verse.

"Come to me, and I will tell you great and unsearchable things you do not know" (Jeremiah 33:3).

So as I lay in bed, overwhelmed by the magical feelings that rush in with a new beginning, I did just that. I went to Jesus. And did He ever tell me great and unsearchable things.

He showed me a picture of myself, sitting on the end of my bed. Kneeling down before me, He handed me a wooden box. "I have a gift for you." He patted the lid. "But you must be willing to give up all of this." He gestured to my room and everything in it. Something stirred within me. I was ready to let go. Of everything. There was nothing in all the earth that I wanted more than Him.

He lifted the lid to the box, and the next thing I saw was a desert, a parched and weary land. Jesus stood beside me and opened His hands before Him. "Forget the former things," He said. "Do not dwell on the past. See, I am doing a new thing! Now it springs up; do you not perceive it? I am making a way in the wilderness and streams in the wasteland" (Isaiah 43:18-19)!

Just then, a stream appeared beside us. He took my hand and led me along the water's edge until we reached the shore of a mighty ocean.

He turned to face me and held both of my tiny hands in His. As His fingers enveloped mine, I noticed the scars–ugly marks that didn't belong on such a beautiful being. They were a remembrance of a wager, a memory of a war, and the promise of a Lord and God who would redeem His people.

I rubbed my thumbs over the marks as He quietly whispered, "The Spirit of the Lord is on me, because He has anointed me to proclaim good news to the poor. He has sent me to proclaim freedom for the prisoners and recovery of sight for the blind, to set the oppressed free, to proclaim the year of the Lord's favor" (Luke 4:18-19). He peered up from our hands and into my eyes. "And now I am sending you."

At that moment, I wasn't exactly sure what Jesus meant, but now I am beginning to understand. I sense Him saying to me, "You have escaped so much, Beloved, but now it is time. It is time for *you* to pick up where I left off. I have anointed you to be the good news to the poor. I am sending you to proclaim freedom for the prisoners and recovery of sight for the blind. You will be the one to set the oppressed free, to proclaim the year of the Lord's favor. I am sending you back, Beloved, back to the prison so you can help the others escape."

Dear precious reader, the Spirit of the Lord is not just on us but in us. God has called us to a life far more radical than the one we are living, a life that is completely antithetical to our old prison cells. We were made to live with His mission. We were made for more!

I, for one, am no longer willing to settle for a life of watered-down, Americanized Christianity. I will stop at nothing but the crazy, radical life of Jesus. I will settle for nothing less than a life buried deep within the story of God.

What about you? Will you come with me? Will this book be for you the steady, patient knocking of Jesus outside your prison cell?

Maybe your door is already open. Then, I urge you, come with me. Come with us.

I stand here boldly beside Jesus, proudly wearing the mission He bore. We have come that you may have life and have it to the full (John 10:10)!

Will you accept the challenge to journey forward? As we extend our hands to you, will you dare to come with us? Hear Him calling out to you, "Come, Beloved. Escape!"+

+ For discussion questions for this chapter, check out page 3 in the complimentary guide *Plan Your ESCAPE*. You can download it for FREE at HeatherRaeHutzel.com/PlanYourEscape

CHAPTER 2

AWAKEN

[uh-wey-kuh n]
verb

1. to awake; waken; to come or bring to an
awareness; to become cognizant
*"Finally, he was awakened to the reality of his
life."*

The morning sun filtered through my bedroom
window and roused me from my sleep. I
stretched, rose from my bed, and walked
down the hall to the kitchen where my family had
gathered around the breakfast table.

"What a strange dream," I said to no one in
particular. "Dreams are so odd, aren't they? Even
though at times they seem real, they feel so very

different from reality." I grabbed my seat and continued. "Being awake is a completely different experience. You can definitely tell the difference between dreams and reality."

I said all this to my family only to actually wake up the next morning and realize my experience was all a dream. The conversation I had with them never happened. It was so bizarre. I was dreaming inside a dream, but when I woke from the first dream, I truly felt and believed I was awake. It seemed like reality.

I decided to do a little research on this phenomenon. The experience of waking inside a dream, or dreaming within a dream, is called a False Awakening. Normally, this experience manifests itself as someone waking (while still in a dream) and going about their daily morning routine as if they were awake. It is not usually the case, though, that someone consciously reasons they are awake, as opposed to merely believing they are awake based on the surroundings and cues in the dream.

My experience made me start to consider the reality in which we live: our state of being awake. Is it possible that everything we tangibly experience on a daily basis is not the true reality? Is our existence upon the earth merely some sort of dream? Are we simply reasoning with ourselves, as I did in my dream, that yes, we are awake when, in fact, we are not? Are we debating the difference between dreams and reality and all the while not actually knowing which one is true? I would argue, yes. The truth is we are living in a state of False Awakening. We are being deceived.

If you have seen the movie *The Matrix*, then you will have an easier time understanding this concept. Our reality is this: we are living in a fictional world.

In the movie *The Matrix*, the people of society were going about their daily lives as free people, not realizing they were actually slaves. Reality, as they experienced it, was a figment of their imagination. Their bodies were locked away, but their minds did not recognize their captivity.

We experience something similar when we dream. Our bodies are immobile, tucked away inside our beds, but our brains continue to roam as if we are not bound by the physical confines of our sleep. Once we wake up, we realize we were only dreaming; everything we experienced wasn't real.

I've come to find that this state of dreaming transcends the realm of physical sleep, especially when it comes to our faith. There is an all-encompassing, pervasive deception that has permeated our world. It has, in a sense, caused us to fall asleep to the true reality of God and His presence. Like the characters in the movie *The Matrix*, we too are living under a false sense of reality, and we are completely oblivious to it.

The Bible makes it very clear that there is a reality we can't see. We are, in a sense, spiritually asleep. Whether you believe it or not, the world we experience on a daily basis is merely the tip of the iceberg of everything that exists. Science proves this to be true. Scientists say that what we, as humans, perceive is only a small fraction of the sounds, scents, and sights in the world around us. Consider dogs. They have an ability to not only hear and smell things we can't, they can also read the energy of humans and other animals. They are able to perceive things as reality that we don't even know exist. Just because we don't believe something to be true, doesn't mean that it isn't. Reality does not conform to our beliefs.

In the same way that a sound may be imperceptible to our human ears, there is a spiritual realm, a land of other worldly beings that intersects with our own. We cannot hear it, see it, or perceive it... most of the time.

The Bible reveals several instances where God "opened the eyes" of His servants, allowing them to see behind the veil. You can read about Balaam, his talking donkey, and the angel of the Lord in Numbers 22:21-35. In 2 Kings 6:8-17, Elisha prayed for God to open the eyes of his servant, so he could see the angelic army that fought on their side.

We will dive into understanding the spiritual realm more fully in future chapters, but for now, know this: there is a God of the universe who created you and has a plan for your life. There is also an enemy who despises you, God, and everything good. This enemy also has a plan for your life: to keep you locked away from God, your Creator, and His perfect love for you.

The enemy of God is crafty, and one of his greatest schemes is making us believe we are awake when we are, in fact, asleep. As in the movie *The Matrix*, many of us believe we are already "free" even though we are still enslaved. We think that because we have proclaimed Jesus as Lord or accepted Him as Savior, it is impossible for us to be held in captivity. After all, we've been "saved." But, friend, there is a very big difference between being free and living free. That's the deception of the enemy.

The adversary has lulled us to sleep and placed in front of us an alternate reality to distract us from the truth. Like a False Awakening (dreaming inside a dream), we are able to be "awakened" or "open our eyes" to this spiritual reality. And it is crucial that we do! There is a war being fought, a spiritual battle that is waged day and night, unseen to the human eye. This battle is for your soul. It is the desire of the enemy to keep you locked inside your prison cell, while God's desire is for you to break free and escape.

How do we wake up? We cannot wake ourselves. It is only through the help of a rescuer, a hero, that we can wake from this dream—Jesus.

The Bible says:

> Their minds were made dull, for to this day the same veil remains... It has not been removed, because only in Christ is it taken away... But whenever anyone turns to the Lord, the veil is taken away. Now the Lord is the Spirit, and where the Spirit of the Lord is, there is freedom. And we all, who with unveiled faces contemplate the Lord's glory, are being transformed into his image with ever-increasing glory, which comes from the Lord, who is the Spirit. (2 Corinthians 3:14-18)

It is only by Jesus Himself or the Spirit of Jesus working through another human being, like my husband, David, that we can wake from our slumber.

The movie *The Matrix* reveals a similar means for breaking free from the machine that held its prisoners in bondage. The people trapped in the Matrix had to "wake up." And it was only through the help of another who was already "awake," a freedom fighter, that they could achieve this enlightened state of freedom.

It's time for us to wake up to the true reality. We are soldiers in a time of war, and there is a mission at hand—to overthrow the enemy and set the captives free!

I want to be your freedom fighter. I want to be the cue in your dream, the glitch in your Matrix, the catalyst that sparks your mind awake, so you can realize you have been living in a fictional world, a story that isn't real. I want to open your eyes to the freedom before you. I want to wake you from the dream that has held you in bondage as a slave. I want to help you escape from living in the wrong story.[+]

> The hour has already come for you to wake up from your slumber, because our salvation is nearer now than when we first believed. The night is nearly over; the day is almost here. (Romans 13:11-12)

+ For discussion questions for this chapter, check out page 4 in the complimentary guide *Plan Your ESCAPE*. You can download it for FREE at HeatherRaeHutzel.com/PlanYourEscape

CHAPTER 3

FICTION

[fik-shuh n]
noun

1. something feigned, invented, or imagined; a
made-up story:
*"Nothing in the story was real. The entire thing was
fiction."*

We are all characters in a story. The question
we must ask ourselves is, "In what story do
we live?"

In this world, there are two main narratives: one
is true, but the other is a work of fiction. As we've
seen, it is the unfortunate reality that many of us,
without even realizing it, have been deceived into
living in the wrong story. I am no exception.

My escape from living in the wrong story began shortly after my "anything" prayer. In the months following that moment when I gave God the "all in" card, the Holy Spirit began to speak to me. He was constantly pointing me in the direction of the books of Genesis and Revelation in the Bible. I was drawn to these two books. I sensed there was a connection the Spirit wanted me to make, but I wasn't sure what it was. I had a gnawing feeling that God had something to say, but the message wasn't clear. Finally, the fog parted, and the missing puzzle piece fell into place.

During my journey of escape, I began listening to talks and sermons from preachers and teachers all around the globe. I was drawn to these "radicals" who taught about the things Jesus said in a context that seemed very different to what I had learned in church growing up. It was one of those sermons that would become the key to unlocking the shackles that still firmly bound my mind.

The spark was ignited while listening to a sermon series called *The Story*. The preacher took a 30,000 foot approach to looking at the Bible, talking about it as one complete story from cover to cover.

In that moment, God began to speak to me. He revealed to me His Story. I was blown away by the details and the mental pictures He was showing me. Words filled my mind as the story was downloaded into my brain. I can remember thinking to myself, "Wow, this should be a book!" And as clear as you can hear someone speaking without actually hearing a voice, God whispered, "Yes, and you are going to write it."

Now, at this point in my life, I had absolutely zero formal writing skills. I was about a year removed from college where I graduated with a business degree. The most writing I ever managed to scrape together was a marketing plan. I hated literature in school and was a mediocre writer at best. I never once had a desire to write anything that wasn't mandatory for passing a class. I am an artist, so I have always been creative when it comes to painting, drawing, and photography. But writing? No way.

God is funny like that, though. He likes to use the least likely or the people who don't have the innate skill set for the calling He has given them. This way, He's the one who shines. Take Moses for example: terrible at speaking and cowardly, yet God asked Him to be the spokesperson for the Israelites living in Egypt. David—a child, a shepherd boy, the least likely to become a warrior or leader: God made him king over Israel and led the nation to countless victories under his rule. Mary—a young, unmarried, peasant girl: God said, "Here, you can be the mother of the Son of God." (Quite the undertaking if you ask me.) Saul—a Christian-killer: God made him into one of the most impactful people for the growing movement called The Way—the disciples and followers of Jesus that Saul once killed.

Now, I am by no means comparing myself to Moses, David, Mary, and Saul, but God clearly has a track record of using people who are the least likely and least qualified. It's all a part of living in His Story. Here's what happens. We *think* we don't have the skill set required for the task God has given us, but instead, we find that God has buried deep within us talents and character traits that He plans to uncover and polish to be used for His glory, if only we will allow Him.

As an artist, God has given me the ability to see things differently than the rest of the world. I had used that talent time and time again to create paintings and photographs, but this time, God made it abundantly clear that I was to paint with words.

Literally minutes after I first sensed God was asking me to write a story, I sat down and started writing. And I kept writing. About an hour later, the first chapter was finished. I read back through what I had written, and it blew my mind. These were not my words.

The really crazy part came soon after. (As if having the God of heaven and earth tell you to write a book isn't strange enough!) A couple days after completing the first chapter of the book, I felt an urge to write again. What God asked me to write this time was not chapter two as you might expect. This time, God revealed to me the very last chapter of the book. It was in that moment I realized, it was no coincidence at all that the Alpha and the Omega, the Beginning and the End, had me write the very first and the very last chapter before anything else.

From there, God began filling in the middle and unfolding the plot of the story, but never could I have imagined the secrets God would reveal to me. Whenever I sat down to write, I would get just as excited as if I were reading a page-turning novel. I had no clue what would come next. It was the most amazing experience of my life. A year and a half later, *The Story of Life* became a published novel.

The Story of Life is a novel based on the words of scripture. It is the story of the Bible told from the unique perspective of the Archangel Michael. In the book, verses from the Bible become the dialogue and narrative of the story as Michael lifts the veil for the reader and reveals everything he has witnessed through the ages: from the beginning when Lucifer rebelled and the spiritual war began, to a modern day world where Michael wages war against the forces of evil and fights for God's plan of redemption.

This is the story that sparked a flame and ignited my passionate inferno for Jesus. This is the book that changed everything and set me on a new course, bound and destined for a life buried deep within the story of God.

Amazingly, stories singlehandedly influence nearly every aspect of our lives. Stories have tremendous power, enabling them to form us and shape us. The story we live in becomes our world view and influences everything: our dreams and aspirations, our actions and consequences, even our identity or the image we portray.

Let me ask you a question, "In which story do you live: one where you're a prisoner, or one where you're a liberated human being?" The character we become is the summation of the story in which we live, and sadly, many of us are living in the wrong story.

The false story that permeates our world manifests itself in many different ways, some of them negative but others seemingly positive. While this fictional story may look like chains of sin and addiction, shackles of greed, or bindings of deceit and lies, more often than not, the fictional story seems harmless, good even. This is the problem with fiction, it isn't real, but it seems like it could be.

Oftentimes, the story of slavery, or as I like to call it, the Story of the World, includes nice sounding things like going to church on Sundays, buying a house, getting married, donating to charities, having kids, getting a promotion, going to college, taking a vacation, inviting friends over for dinner, and retirement.

Now, you may ask, "What's wrong with these things? What is wrong with getting married and buying a home? What is the problem with wanting to get a promotion or rise through the ranks at work?" And my answer is, "Nothing." There is nothing inherently wrong with these major life events. Like most people, I can check many of them off the list. The problem does not lie within these individual events but rather in the motivation behind these events.

Let me tell you about a little thing called the "American Dream." The American Dream begins at birth and follows a person to their death. It includes notions such as life, liberty, and the pursuit of happiness. This philosophy centers on upward mobility, prosperity, hard work, and the need to overcome as few hurdles as possible to achieving such. The American Dream speaks of all men being equal. It boasts of our right to opportunity, success, and achievement. It is the dream of a life full of riches and happiness and devoid of struggles and sacrifice. This is the American Dream; it is a chapter in the Story of the World. For a long time, I thought this was my dream and my story.

The biggest problem I see with the Story of the World is this: it centers on ME. The motivation behind my decisions is based on what benefits me. What do *I* want? What do *I* like? What will be best for *me* and *my* family? How can *I* get ahead? How can *I* feel good about *myself*? Will this job be a good move for *me* and *my* kids? Is this church a good fit for *me*? Will this house be a good investment for *my* future? The list goes on.

We need to realize, we are *not* supposed to be the main characters of our story or any story. God is. Our lives are merely sentences, lines of a paragraph lost among the pages of a much grander story.

In his book *The Irresistible Revolution*, Shane Claiborne says, "The world cannot afford the American Dream and the good news is that there is another dream." I want you to know that you cannot afford the Story of the World. The price is too steep. It will drain you of every resource you have and deprive you of the opportunity to fulfill your God-given purpose. Even worse, the Story of the World will cost you your soul. The good news is there is another story, and you were made to be a part of it.

The problem with the Story of the World is that we experience it on a daily basis. It permeates our lives. Most of us don't even recognize it. This fictional story has become the air we breathe and the water in which we swim. It is the life we experience. It seems normal. It seems right. But so do dreams when we are asleep.

As Leonardo di Caprio's character in the movie *Inception* so eloquently said, "Dreams feel real while we're in them. It's only when we wake up that we realize something was actually strange."

So too with our captivity. Without even realizing, we have nestled ourselves in among the pages of this false story. It's as if we have fallen asleep.

Dear reader, it's time for us to wake up and realize that like the proverbial Alice in Wonderland, we too are lost in the wrong story. Though we are not the main character, our lives do have a purpose. There is a reason for our existence as human beings. We have an incredibly important role to play in the real story. And let me say, it is the best story, the greatest story. In fact, it's the greatest story ever told.[+]

+ For discussion questions for this chapter, check out page 5 in the complimentary guide *Plan Your ESCAPE*. You can download it for FREE at HeatherRaeHutzel.com/PlanYourEscape

CHAPTER 4

TRUTH

[trooth]
noun

1. the true or actual state of a matter; conformity
with fact or reality; verity:
*"I can't believe it; all these years, I've never known
the truth."*

I'd like to ask you to do something that, for some
of us, will prove to be very difficult. Heck, it
might even feel impossible, but for the remainder
of this book, I want you to attempt to forget
everything you know about God and the Bible.
Imagine this is your first time hearing God's Story.
For some of us, this won't be difficult at all. It

really depends on how familiar we already are with God's Story.

Familiarity is one of our biggest hindrances when it comes to understanding God and His Story. It's one of the heaviest chains we bear. Familiarity waters down the extraordinary and makes it seem ordinary. God's Story is absolutely anything but ordinary, so let's do this together. Cast off those chains of familiarity and curl up in a comfy spot. It's story time.

In the beginning, God created the heavens and the earth (Genesis 1:1). In six days, He created the earth and all that is in it, and on the seventh day He rested from His work. This is the beginning according to the Bible. But do you want to know something interesting? It's not truly the beginning.

God is infinite. He has no beginning and no end. In fact, the Bible tells us that God *is* the beginning and the end. So if God Himself has no beginning and no end, then His Story also has no beginning and no end. The question then becomes, why does the Bible mark Genesis 1:1 as "The Beginning?"

It's quite simple actually. That's where God *decided* to begin telling His Story. And when we take into consideration God's infiniteness, when and where God chooses to begin telling His Story becomes incredibly revealing about His character. God chose the moment of creation to begin the unfolding of this epic tale, and there is something very significant about the beginning of creation: it's the beginning of us!

God's Story is a love story, and God chose the starting point of His Story to be the moment we walked onto the scene, the moment He created us. It's as if He is saying, "There is no story worth telling before I met you."

As we delve into the story of God, we see that this character of overwhelming love is spilled all over the pages of the Bible. This story, the Bible, is about the greatest lover who ever lived and the object of His adoration—you.

The story revolves around God (He's the main character, after all), yet His love for us is so great that He makes us feel like everything is about us. He dotes on us, creating an entire universe of stars and planets, seas filled with unfathomable delights, towering mountains, deep valleys, and flowers that capture more hues than a rainbow. God's love is so radical that He wants to make us feel as though the universe revolves around us, when, truly, it revolves around Him. God is crazy about us.

This all-loving, crazy-about-us kind of God reveals Yahweh's true character. God's identity is not found in the titles He bears such as King, Lord Almighty, or Creator of the Heavens and the Earth. Yes, He is the Alpha and the Omega, the Beginning and the End, and nothing is too great or too small for Him. It's true that He is the self-existent and self-sustaining one, who has no origin though we and all of creation do. God always was and always will be. There is nothing He needs in order to sustain His existence, and there is nothing He needs in order to propagate His will. God is God; that is His nature, but it is not His character.

1 John 4:8 gives us a very complete and profound description of the character of God; it

says, "God is love." This is who God is. We think of love as a verb, as in "I love my husband" or "I love my parents, brother, and dog." But the Bible tells us, love is not merely the verb that God does, no, it is also the noun that He is.

According to pastor and theologian Greg Boyd, love is defined as, "ascribing unsurpassable worth to another at cost to oneself." The Bible gives us the exact same definition but phrases it this way: "This is how we know what love is, Jesus Christ laid down his life for us. And we ought to lay down our lives for one another" (1 John 3:16).

Whatever definition of love you subscribe to, love by its very nature requires two or more parties to be involved. Since we know that love is not simply the verb that God does but also the noun that He is, we can correctly assume that God, at His very core, exists in a form of more than one party: Father, Son, and Holy Spirit. These three relate to one another in a constant, flowing existence, exchanging value and worth to one another.

In the eternity before God created human beings, He existed as the Three In One, loving perfectly among Himself. But God intended for that love to be shared and for His Kingdom and story to expand. This is the very reason God created humankind upon the earth in the first place, because He was so full of love, He wanted to spread it and share it.

Imagine for a moment what it would look like to fill a water balloon at your sink. You stretch the balloon over the faucet, turn on the water, and the balloon begins to fill. You leave the water running, and the balloon continues to grow and expand and get bigger until finally… POP! Water and pieces of rubber go everywhere! This is how I picture God's love.

In the beginning, God was so completely full of the most perfect kind of love that He couldn't contain Himself. He had to share it! He was, quite literally *dying* to love us!

From the moment of our inception, God has been pouring Himself out for us. Genesis 2:7 perfectly illustrates the beauty of this kind of crazy love. It says, "Then the Lord God formed a man from the dust of the ground and breathed into his nostrils the breath of life, and the man became a living being."

Now perhaps nothing particularly breathtaking jumped out at you when you read this verse. I urge you; read it again. Read it with skin on. Use your imagination to see what was really happening. This is a story after all. Go there with me.

Picture it: the Lord God Almighty, the Creator of the heavens and the earth, slowly stooping down, kneeling into the dust and dirt of the planet He created. He reaches forward into the mud with His strong masculine hands and begins forming, shaping, and creating a figure… a figure that looks just like Him. Finally, He finishes His work, sits back onto His heels, and wipes the sweat from His brow. He takes in the beauty of His most prized creation, but it just lays before Him cold, lifeless, and still. But God has a plan. He leans forward, getting as close as possible, smiling as He considers what He is about to do. That's when it happens. He breathes into His creation's nostrils the breath of life, and it is at *that* moment that the man becomes a living being.

The Bible tells us that God is life, so when God breathed into Adam the breath of life, He breathed Himself or His Spirit into him. God placed His very existence inside of Adam.

Genesis 1:27 says, "God created mankind in his image, in the image of God he created them, male and female he created them."

God originally created humans not only to look like Him but to live like Him and be like Him. We were to be God's ambassadors upon the earth and bring all creation under our authority. We were created to be an extension of God's love, to be an extension of God Himself. But something happened.

As I mentioned earlier, the creation account in Genesis is not truly the beginning. It is merely the place where God chose to begin telling His Story. We can tell from scripture that sometime before God ever created humans, He created a heavenly realm filled with angelic beings.

One of those angelic beings was Lucifer, a guardian cherub who is described as being full of wisdom and perfect in beauty (Ezekiel 28:12). The Bible tells us he "became proud on account of his beauty" and "corrupted his wisdom because of his splendor" (Ezekiel 28:17).

Lucifer desired the praise and adoration that was given to God. So he rebelled, and in the process, succeeded in taking a portion of God's angelic warriors with him, creating an opposing spiritual army. On the day God banished Lucifer from Heaven, he became the adversary, Satan, and a great war began—a war between good and evil, a battle between truth and fiction.

God never meant for there to be any other story than the one He was writing, but because both humans and angelic beings were given free will, there became the possibility for something other than God's perfect and beautiful tale. As the story goes, Satan disguised himself as a serpent, tempting Adam and Eve. And they sinned, bringing a curse upon the entire human race and ultimately upon the image of God.

God never meant for us to get caught up in the Story of the World. The war was His, but by our own volition, we humans chose to become a part of the battle. We opted in. Adam and Eve became caught up in the war between God and Satan, choosing to know evil when God wanted to shelter them from it in the paradise He called Eden.

Lucifer and his followers used their free will and chose to rebel, creating evil. We chose to disobey, opening our eyes to that evil.

Now don't think for one second that this story is just history and that Adam and Eve were the ones who screwed up the entire world. Every day is a choice for us. Will we choose to remain in Eden, in the story of God? Or will we choose a different story, a tempting fictional one that perhaps looks appealing but is filled with war, pain, and suffering?

The real irony of the story is the ploy Satan used to tempt Adam and Eve. Satan told them that when they ate the fruit from the tree of the knowledge of good and evil, they would be *like* God. The truth is they were already like God! God made them in His image!

This is how Satan tempts and deceives us. He convinces us that the true story is the one that isn't real. He tells us we are not really awake in order to lull us to sleep and place in front of us an alternate reality. Satan has convinced us that there is no war, there is no spiritual realm, and there is no need to worry. So we go about our lives unaware and oblivious to the fact that we are slaves locked inside the wrong story. But we were made for a different story—a story where we are not slaves but an army of conquerors, no, MORE than conquerors (Romans 8:37). But, friend, let me ask you, "What's God to do with an army that is fast asleep inside their prison cells?"

As we dive deeper into the story of God, one thing will become incredibly apparent: we have been deceived. John 8:44 describes Satan as the "father of lies." The verse says, "When he lies, he speaks his native language."

This is what Satan does now and has been doing since the beginning. Humanity's very first interaction with our enemy in the Garden of Eden resulted in us believing the deception he placed before us, creating an alternate reality—the fictional story.

Deception is a very dangerous thing. By its nature, deceit is tricky and difficult to discern. This is why True or False tests are so challenging. On one hand, you have pretty good odds for guessing correctly, but on the other hand, one small change to a factual statement can render it null and void. You have to read the statements very carefully to ensure nothing was slipped in to change the meaning and truthfulness of the words.

This is the nature of Satan. Like a teacher who cleverly rearranges the words on a True or False exam, our enemy, in his craftiness, takes the words of God and twists them ever so slightly, giving them a new and incorrect meaning.

2 Corinthians 4:4 says, "The god of this age [Satan] has blinded the minds of unbelievers, so that they cannot see the light of the gospel that displays the glory of Christ, who is the image of God."

Satan told Adam and Eve that when they ate from the tree of the knowledge of good and evil, their eyes would be opened, but what he didn't tell them is that, in a sense, they would also be blinded. Their eyes were opened to one reality, but closed to another.

God's story was the only thing Adam and Eve could see before the fall, but now their vision was clouded with elements of fiction and deceit, things that didn't matter in comparison to the relationship they once had with God.

Through his clever deception, Satan destroyed the two foundational pieces of God's Story. He altered the way we view God's character, and he wrecked our understanding of our own identity. These are the core elements of the story. God's Story hinges on us understanding these two components: God's character and our identity. That is why the process of escaping our slavery depends on us first understanding the story.

Take a minute to read the following verses from Genesis 3.

Now the serpent was more crafty than any of the wild animals the Lord God had made. He said to the woman, "Did God really say, 'You must not eat from any tree in the garden'?"

The woman said to the serpent, "We may eat fruit from the trees in the garden, but God did say, 'You must not eat fruit from the tree that is in the middle of the garden, and you must not touch it, or you will die.'"

"You will not certainly die," the serpent said to the woman. "For God knows that when you eat from it your eyes will be opened, and you will be like God, knowing good and evil." (Genesis 3:1-5)

When Satan tempted Adam and Eve, he planted a lie about the character of God, causing the humans to question God's goodness. He caused them to wonder, "Does God really love us like He says He does, or is He holding out on us?"

How many times do we ask the very same question?

The second lie Satan told was about the identity of Adam and Eve. Satan made it sound like Adam and Eve weren't already *like* God. But they were! The truth is that Adam and Eve were actually less like God after eating the fruit that God commanded them not to eat.

When God created the first man and woman, they were, indeed, very special. They were made in the image and very likeness of God! That was the intent for the entire human race. Unfortunately, God's intent was not the fate that befell humankind. By the free will given to them, Adam and Eve chose sin and subjected creation to a curse. As a result, they felt shame and began to cover themselves, not only physically but spiritually and emotionally. The race of people that began to populate the earth was one of greed, secrecy, wrath, lust, and deceit. They no longer bore the resemblance of their Creator as they once had.

Now herein lies the very reason I believe we, as humans, do not understand the character of God. If we, who were once supposed to reflect the character and essence of God, no longer bear His image, then how in the world are we supposed to know the true character of God?

We are hardwired to draw a connection between God's character and our human character. This tendency is deeply ingrained in our DNA by the Creator Himself, originally meant for good. Yet it is because of this fact that we make the fatal error of attaching our human flaws to God, corrupting His perfect character. We look to ourselves and to each other and apply the same qualities we see in our fellow humans to the character of God.

Before the curse, we mirrored God's character and He mirrored ours. Now, the reflection we offer is a sin-stained version of humanity. This is the image we project back on God. This is why so many of us, myself included, end up with such a warped picture of God. People believe God is untrustworthy because we can't trust our neighbor. People believe they have to earn God's love because that is how we obtain the love of family and friends. This is why some people aren't even sure God exists, because in a world of deceit and secrecy, where everyone hides their true identity, no one knows what is real anymore.

We are all guilty of misrepresenting the character of God, even if it is only in the deep recesses of our souls where we question His intentions. God made us in His image, but we have to remember, in a fallen and sinful state, we no longer reflect that perfect image.

Before their downfall, Adam and Eve were different. They were untainted, created by the very hands of God, crafted perfectly in His image. They had the Spirit of the living God inside them. They were an extension of God, one with Him in every way, but the serpent convinced them that something was missing from their identity, that they weren't who God said they were.[+]

In an attempt to overthrow and attack an all-powerful, unconquerable God, Satan hit Him the only place where He was vulnerable—His heart. Satan twisted the dagger by separating God from a piece of Himself, the thing He loved and needed most.

Have you ever considered that God needs you? Sounds like a pretty radical statement (almost blasphemous, really), but the fictional Story of the

---

+ Read more about identity on page 6 of the complimentary guide *Plan Your ESCAPE*. You can download it for FREE at HeatherRaeHutzel.com/PlanYourEscape

World has clouded our vision, obscuring the beauty of the true character of God.

While it is true that God doesn't need us, in the sense that we in some way contribute to His existence, God does need us in the sense that we might say, "I need my spouse." God created us as a piece of Himself so that not only would we need Him but that He also would need us. When we were torn from Him, it was like having a part of His body severed from the whole.

When the King of kings came to earth in human flesh and died a God-forsaken death, He wasn't saying, "I can't exist without you," He was saying, "I don't want to exist without you." His actions became a declaration that screamed, "I want you so desperately that it feels like a need. If death is where you are, then that is where I'll go! I don't want to live without you!"

Some people think that saying God needs someone or something belittles His power or demeans His authority in some way. Yet there is something supremely more awesome about a King who chooses to exercise His power in the way God does.

1 Corinthians 1 says, "...the message of the cross is foolishness to those who are perishing, but to us who are being saved it is the power of God... For the foolishness of God is wiser than human wisdom, and the weakness of God is stronger than human strength" (v. 18 & 25). These are not just some nice-sounding words we find in scripture. Paul even says in verse 17, "For Christ did not send me to baptize, but to preach the gospel—not with

wisdom and eloquence, lest the cross of Christ be emptied of its power."

God's Kingdom is not of this world (John 18:36); therefore, the way God reveals His power is not the way we might think. God fights for us in a revolutionary, upside down kind of way. God's power is found on the cross—radical, self-sacrificial love and the desire for us to become one with Him. This is the power of God.

God is not vulnerable by nature, but because of His loving character, He chooses to become vulnerable. God laid His heart on the line when He created human beings with free will. He gave us the ability to choose something other than Him, but He also gave us the choice to partner with Him. God created us to participate in manifesting His Kingdom through work and prayer. God created us so He could delight in our existence and the things we achieve for His Kingdom. God wanted us to choose Him above everything else. He wanted us to love Him the way that He loves us. He created us to be a part of the story He was telling with all creation, but as you've seen, we have chosen a very different path.

The amazing part of the story is that God did not abandon Adam and Eve as He could have so rightfully done. He did not cast them from the garden because He was so disgusted by their sin. No. The reason He cast them from the garden was so they couldn't also take and eat from the tree of life and live forever in their fallen and sinful state. God's banishment of Adam and Eve was an act of mercy. He loved them. He needed them, but as a pure Holy God, nothing could be a part of Him that was blemished and stained. There was only one thing He could do.

So as Adam and Eve hung their heads and somberly made their way out of the garden, God turned to Satan and said, "I want them back."[+]

"You want them back?" Satan spat. "You cannot have them back. They belong to me now. The cost to get them back would be too steep. There is no price you could pay!"

As these words left Satan's lips, a hush fell over the garden as God turned to him and said, "No price is too great for My created ones whom I love. To be with them, I would do anything."

From here, God's Story continues, but the plot takes an astonishing turn.[+]

[+] God wants you. Read this short story on page 9 of the complimentary guide *Plan Your ESCAPE*. Discussion questions for this chapter are on page 13. You can download the guide for FREE at HeatherRaeHutzel.com/PlanYourEscape

CHAPTER 5

VILLAIN

[vil-uh n]
noun

1. a cruelly malicious person who is involved in or devoted to wickedness or crime; a character in a novel who constitutes an important evil agency in the plot:
"The villain's wickedness was surpassed only by his charm and deceit."

When we are children, fairy tales are the stories that shape our worldview. We believe in magic, we are convinced fairies are real, and we have a genuine fear of the monsters under our bed. But what happens as we get older?

Our parents break it to us as gently as possible: Santa and the Tooth Fairy aren't real, and they assure us there is no such thing as monsters under the bed. Our entire worldview is flipped upside down. As a result we grow up; we stop believing in magic and the supernatural. We discover and accept that these are the elements of folklore, fantasy, and fiction.

So perhaps it is not surprising that when we are introduced to a concept like spiritual warfare, it is difficult for some of us to grasp. Compared to other cultures, our science-minded, Western beliefs are mostly devoid of anything paranormal or supernatural. To this point, even certain Bible stories have been watered down because they seem too fanciful.

If we were to remove every supernatural or non-physical event from the Bible, there honestly wouldn't be much left. We need to stop reading the Bible through the lens of our Western culture.

We can try to explain away the things that seem too strange or enigmatic, but the fact remains, just because we don't believe something to be true, doesn't mean that it isn't. We don't know and can't know everything about God and the Bible. His thoughts and ways are not ours; they are higher and greater (Isaiah 55:8-9).

Let's face it. There are things in the Bible we can't explain. Some things, no theologian, scientist, or historian can explain. And you know what? We should be okay with that. Our faith should not be challenged by our lack of understanding. If we can explain everything about God, then He is not God.

Our faith should be more challenged by a God we can fully explain than by a God who remains in so many ways a mystery.

If there is one thing I've learned over the last several years, it's that I can't learn everything about God. The more I come to know about Him and His Story, the more I realize just how little I know.

God's story is amazing. It is completely mind-blowing! And once we move beyond the tamed version of the stories we are taught as children, we will realize, "This is one crazy book!" I encourage you to take comfort in the fact that we can't know everything, because our God does, and He is the one writing this story.

When we set aside our Western glasses and really dive into the story, one thing becomes incredibly apparent: the Bible references spiritual warfare far more than we realize. In fact, this war zone is the setting and stage for the entire story.

God's Story is not just a story of love. It is also a story of war—a war between good and evil, a battle between truth and fiction. A story about two diabolically opposed kingdoms featuring a good King and an evil villain.

You've already had a brief introduction to the enemy in our story, but now we are going to get to know him a little better. We need to understand our enemy if we are going to expose his plan of attack.

As we've seen, scripture tells us that God is not the only spiritual being in existence. Before God created humans, He created a heavenly realm filled with other, but lesser, celestial beings. As you know, one of those beings was Lucifer who we would later call Satan.

Lucifer was an incredibly beautiful and wise angelic being. Ezekiel 28:12 describes him as "the seal of perfection, full of wisdom and perfect in beauty." So what happened? How could a being that dwelt with the Almighty Himself become so evil and wicked? How could he fall so far? It's an easy answer—free will.

Like human beings, celestial beings were also given free will. *Real* love requires a choice. Unfortunately, a number of these spiritual creatures would eventually choose to turn against God and His plan in order to fulfill their own self-serving desires. Lucifer was not the only one who would use his free will to meddle with God's plan for humanity, but he was the first.

As the story goes, Lucifer became proud because of his elite status. He desired more and began yearning after the glory bestowed upon the King. He chose to allow his pride and greed to get the best of him and abandoned his Lord. The Bible says wickedness was found in him (Ezekiel 28:15). He became proud on account of his beauty.

Isaiah 14:13-14 references Lucifer as saying:

"I will ascend to the heavens;
I will raise my throne
    above the stars of God;
I will sit enthroned on the mount of assembly,
    on the utmost heights of Mount Zaphon.
I will ascend above the tops of the clouds;

I will make myself like the Most High."

Ezekiel chapter twenty-eight rounds out the story with God saying:

Through your widespread trade
    you were filled with violence,
    and you sinned.
So I drove you in disgrace from the mount
of God,
    and I expelled you, guardian cherub,
    from among the fiery stones.
Your heart became proud
    on account of your beauty,
and you corrupted your wisdom
    because of your splendor.
So I threw you to the earth;
    I made a spectacle of you before kings.
(vv. 16-17)

This was the moment sin was birthed. The reason God banished Lucifer from Heaven was because Lucifer became the very thing that God was not.

In the previous chapter, we talked about God's character. We said God is love, and we defined love as ascribing unsurpassable worth to another at cost to ourselves. This is who God is at the core of His essence.

But let's take a look at something. What happens if we reverse the definition of love? It looks like this: the opposite of love is to ascribe unsurpassable *worth to yourself* at *cost to another*.

This behavior is the contrasting antithesis of love and the farthest thing from God. It goes by many different names: pride, arrogance, self-centeredness, haughtiness, but perhaps the most appropriate is this: selfish ambition.

Selfish means devoted to or caring only for oneself; concerned primarily with one's own interests, benefits, and welfare, regardless of others. The definition of ambition is an earnest desire for some type of achievement or distinction, as in power, honor, fame, or wealth, and the willingness to strive for its attainment. Therefore, selfish ambition can be described this way: the willingness to strive for one's own interests, benefits, and welfare, at a cost to others.

Selfish ambition is an ugly, ugly beast and a dangerous one at that. James 3:16 has this to say about it, "For where you have envy and selfish ambition, there you find disorder and every evil practice."

As Mark Batterson says in his book *All In*, "At its core, sinfulness is selfishness. It's enthroning yourself—your desires, your needs, your plans—above all else."[1]

Selfish ambition was the downfall of Lucifer, and it was the downfall of humankind. God created humans in His image to reflect His love, but as we'll see in the next chapter, anything that is not congruent with God's loving character cannot remain in His presence.

Love is the greatest force in the universe. It is

---

1. Batterson, Mark. *All In: You Are One Decision Away from a Totally Different Life*. Grand Rapids, MI: Zondervan, 2013.

what propels existence. It is the through-line of God's Story and the very foundation upon which He builds. There is nothing greater than love.

"And now these three remain: faith, hope and love. But the greatest of these is love" (1 Corinthians 13:13).

Love is a force; it is the force that defines God, and it is the motive and purpose for all creation. God created so He could expand the love that already existed within Him.

Think about it this way: God created human beings in His image; therefore, we were created in the image of love. We were made to be an extension of the love that God is. This means, when God created humankind, He made us out of love so that we, in our relationships with God and with each other, would exactly replicate the love that flows endlessly between the Father, Son, and Holy Spirit. Our very essence, our makeup, our DNA was made to be the same as God's—LOVE!

Love has a flow to it, a natural course of motion that, when working properly, benefits all creation in the best way possible. This is why Jesus, when asked, "What is the greatest commandment?" responded like this:

> 'Love the Lord your God with all your heart and with all your soul and with all your mind.' This is the first and greatest commandment. And the second is like it: 'Love your neighbor as yourself.' All the Law and the Prophets hang on these two commandments. (Matthew 22:37-40)

Love is a force to be poured out. We pour out our love toward God, we pour out our love toward others, and in return, they pour out their love into us. Love is something that is meant to be poured into and poured out of us that we may constantly be filled with new love.

Consider for a moment the way water flows in nature. Rain pours down and floods a stream; the stream flows to the river; the river empties into the ocean; the ocean water evaporates into the air so that it may once again pour down as rain. As a result, everyone benefits from this type of system: humans, animals, and plants. Now, let me ask you a question. "What happens to a body of water that is enclosed?" Right, it becomes stagnant. So too with love.

In the region of the world where Jesus lived and conducted His ministry, there are two very different bodies of water: the Sea of Galilee and the Dead Sea. The Sea of Galilee has water that flows into it from an external source, but it also pours out its resources into another body of water. Because of this healthy ecosystem, the Sea of Galilee is teeming with aquatic life. In comparison, the Dead Sea also has water that flows into it from an external source, but unlike the Sea of Galilee, it does *not* empty into another body of water. As a result, the Dead Sea has sodium levels that are so high, nothing can live in it.

Selfish ambition is essentially self-love. It is placing ourselves above others. Now, you might be thinking, "But Jesus said to love our neighbor as ourselves. His words imply that we must love ourselves first, right?"

Yes, but also, no. A more accurate way to read Jesus' words may be, "Love your neighbor instead of yourself. Love them the way you would love yourself or would want to be loved."

Love is taking the value and worth that you have and giving it away. You cannot love yourself and love another at the same time. Love is a zero sum game. Jesus demonstrated this perfectly on the cross. In fact, what Jesus did was so profound, the Bible equates His actions with the very definition of love. "This is how we know what love is: Jesus Christ laid down his life for us. And we ought to lay down our lives for our brothers and sisters" (1 John 3:16).

Selfish ambition, or self-love, is a way of placing ourselves above God. This is the crime for which Lucifer is guilty—the same sin Adam and Eve committed.

Anytime we do not obey what God commands us, we are placing ourselves above God. The Bible tells us in John 14:21, "Whoever has my commands and obeys them is the one who loves me." When we intentionally disobey God, we are clearly placing our own comfort or our desires above His. If we disobey out of a lack of trust, we are still elevating ourselves, because we are essentially saying that we think our way is better than God's.

Lucifer's selfish ambition took over when, in his own mind, he intentionally elevated himself to the position that only God maintains. Adam and Eve did the same thing when they decided they wanted to become "like" God, not trusting or believing that they were already like God and that He knew what was best for them. They reflected Him perfectly in the way they loved until the moment they turned that love away from God. In disobedience, they placed their own desires above His. That was the moment they stopped reflecting God's image.

You know, I've often wondered why the very first human sin was something, seemingly, so minor—eating a piece of forbidden fruit, the apparent equivalent of stealing a cookie from a cookie jar. The truth lies in what we just unveiled. It wouldn't have mattered what the infraction was. Any deviation from the pure, all holy, all loving, self-sacrificial, other-oriented love of God would be enough to separate us from Him forever, for "all have sinned and fall short of the glory of God" (Romans 3:23).

***

Unfortunately, this war has become the framework for the world we live in today. It is a part of the story that is being told with our lives. This battle between good and evil continues to permeate our existence. I don't have to tell you this. You know from looking around and seeing the pain and suffering that floods our world. This is how we know that the world in which we live is broken. This is how we know that, somewhere along the way, the story has gone off script. Fortunately, our God is still the God of love, and His desire is still for us to be like Him. And while our story may have been broken, thankfully, the Main Character is also the Author, and He has already rewritten the plot.[+]

+ For discussion questions for this chapter, check out page 14 in the complimentary guide *Plan Your ESCAPE*. You can download it for FREE at HeatherRaeHutzel.com/PlanYourEscape

CHAPTER 6

EDIT

[ed-it]
verb

1. to revise or correct, as a manuscript:
"The story originally had a horrible ending, but the author decided to edit the final chapter."

"Holy, holy, holy is the Lord God Almighty, who was and is and is to come" (Revelation 4:8).

Holy: otherworldly, different, unique. Set-apart, strange, ethereal. Supernatural, matchless, exceptional. Holy.

If there is one thing you need to know about God, it's that He is holy. Holy smokes, is He ever holy. He is set-apart in this way. He is unlike us.

The Bible says in 1 Timothy 6:16 that He dwells in unapproachable light. None can look upon His face and live. None can enter into His presence and withstand. He is holy, good, and loving, and anything that is not holy, good, and loving cannot survive in His presence.

In a previous chapter, we discovered it was not God's desire to be separated from Adam and Eve, but it was necessary. Adam and Eve lost their holiness when they sinned, so God cast them from His presence.

From the moment God first breathed His life into us, He already knew there was a chance we would abandon Him. He also knew He would never abandon us because "love believes all things and hopes all things," (1 Corinthians 13:7 ESV). God set before us life and death, blessings and curses, believing and hoping we would choose life and live (Deuteronomy 30:19). Yet at the same time, He already knew He loved us enough to die for us. God already had a plan put in place, and now it was time to edit the story.

***

In the same way that darkness cannot exist in the presence of light, anything that is not like God cannot exist in His presence. When light pierces the dark, what can the night do but flee? Even one tiny spark of light, one flicker of a candle is enough to eradicate darkness. Because darkness is simply the absence of all light, it cannot remain when in the presence of anything illuminating. This is us. In contrast to God's holiness, we are darkness.

When we examine God's Story, we see that, by our own choice and free will, humanity as a whole chose a path that was different from God. We once were light (filled with the presence of God), but we chose to become darkness (void of His Spirit). As darkness, we cannot exist in the all-holy light of God's presence.

God can't be in the company of unholiness, because it is not what He is. He is holy. At the same time, unholiness can't exist in the attendance of God. This is why God banished Adam and Eve from the Garden of Eden when they ate the fruit from the Tree of the Knowledge of Good and Evil. God banished them as an act of mercy.

If we ate from the Tree of Life, we would live forever as unholy beings, creatures that could never enter into the presence of God without being destroyed. Not because God wanted to destroy us, but because He couldn't help it. Our destruction would be the natural consequence of being unholy humans in the presence of a God who is holy. If Adam and Eve remained in His presence, they would perish.

Through the deception of the enemy (Satan) and our own disobedience, we humans locked ourselves away inside the prison of our unholiness and sin. Thus, humanity was separated from God. We thrust ourselves into a different story.

The Bible tells us God is life. In the same way that darkness is the absence of light, death is the absence of life. And if God is life, then the absence of God is death.

When Adam and Eve violated God's design and His created order, they allowed natural and destructive consequences to enter their lives and the lives of all their descendants. The natural consequence of unholiness is separation from God—ultimately death. It has to happen. Adam and Eve would either die immediately in the unquenchable fire of God's holiness or die because they were separated from His presence.

Like Adam and Eve, we too would be extinguished in the presence of the Lord God Almighty if it weren't for the sacrifice Jesus already made. The pieces of us that are unlike God make us unclean. We are not like Him. We are not good. We are not holy. Therefore, in the presence of the Holy One, we perish. Unless we have the Spirit of God inside us while on earth, technically, we are dead. Ephesians 2:1-2 says, "As for you, you were dead in your transgressions and sins, in which you used to live when you followed the ways of this world and of the ruler of the kingdom of the air, the spirit who is now at work in those who are disobedient."

At the fall of mankind, in a real spiritual sense, humanity became imprisoned, locked away from the presence of God so we would not be destroyed. God sent us out of His presence because of His great love for us, so that in His infinite wisdom, He could make a way back.

The only way we can ever stand in the presence of God again is to be holy as He is holy. To be spotless, blameless, set-apart, different, and otherworldly. But how can we as humans be holy? Every sin, every stain, every piece of us that is unlike God is another chain that binds us to our prison cell where, without a savior, we will rot and die. Each chain is like a weight around our neck, making it seem as though our escape is impossible. Even if the door was unlocked, how could we ever flee the prison cell with the shackles of unholiness bound securely around our hands and feet?

There is ONLY ONE who is holy, God Himself. There is NO other. The only hope for our escape, the only way for us to be back in the presence of our King is to be holy as He is holy. As we will see, this became a very impossible task to achieve.

***

God has always been trying to make us more like Him, to be holy as He is holy. This is the theme of the entire Old Testament.

After the fall of humanity, a great chasm existed between us and our Creator, something many of us still experience today. There is a longing inside us to be with God as we once were in Eden, but somehow we know we are too broken to come before Him. Something that has been wronged needs to be righted.

After being cast from the garden, the Bible tells us that Adam and Eve had two sons: Cain and Abel. We aren't given much detail about their lives, but the little we do have is a bit puzzling. Let's take a quick look at the text and dive into the next part of God's Story.

Adam made love to his wife Eve, and she became pregnant and gave birth to Cain. She said, "With the help of the Lord I have brought forth a man." Later she gave birth to his brother Abel.

Now Abel kept flocks, and Cain worked the soil. In the course of time Cain brought some of the fruits of the soil as an offering to the Lord. And Abel also brought an offering—fat portions from some of the firstborn of his flock. The Lord looked with favor on Abel and his offering, but on Cain and his offering he did not look with favor. So Cain was very angry, and his face was downcast.

Then the Lord said to Cain, "Why are you angry? Why is your face downcast? If you do what is right, will you not be accepted? But if you do not do what is right, sin is crouching at your door; it desires to have you, but you must rule over it." (Genesis 4:1-7)

As the story goes, Cain gave into his anger and murdered his own brother, perpetuating the sin and curse his parents brought upon creation.

But here is the perplexing question: why did God accept Abel's sacrifice and not Cain's? The best answer I've heard was given in a three part sermon series entitled *The End of Religion.*[+]

[+] You can find links to this sermon series on page 15 of the complimentary guide *Plan Your ESCAPE*. You can download it for FREE at HeatherRaeHutzel.com/PlanYourEscape

The pastor, Bruxy Cavey, explains the text this way: God made a declaration back in Genesis 3 that, one day, the offspring of the woman would crush the head of the enemy. When reading this text today, we re-read Jesus back into God's promise, but Adam and Eve had no context for doing so. They had no reason *not* to believe that their firstborn, Cain, would be the one to make things right for them. The text even places emphasis on Cain as opposed to Abel.

Cain probably grew up hearing stories about how his parents were banished from the garden, but that one day, he would be the one to make things right. In an attempt to right things with God, Cain took matters into his own hands and came up with a brilliant plan—Cain would give God back His fruit.

From what we can tell in scripture, God didn't ask Cain and Abel for sacrifices and offerings. The boys seemingly gave out of their own free will. While Abel gave an offering to God out of joy and gratitude, Cain's gift was given as a way to make amends, a way to bridge the gap. The text says nothing to make us think God was angry with Cain for making this offering, just that He did not look on it with favor.

God is not looking for us to sacrifice or perform or follow rules or keep observances in order to be in relationship with Him. Don't believe me? Check out what God said to Cain, "If you do what is right, will you not be accepted?" He was saying, "Cain, just be who I created you to be, My image bearer. Live according to the love I have shown you."

But Cain would not have it. Cain was the one who became angry, not God. The mindset of religion took over. He felt justified, and in his self-righteous attitude, he pitted himself against his own brother. Religious indignation became the motivation for the very first murder, and sadly, it would not be the last.

From here, the beautiful story that God began writing continues to spin wildly out of control with stories of greed, war, deceit, murder, disobedience, and even strange occurrences of angelic beings cohabiting and reproducing with human women.[+]

With free-will beings as characters in God's Story, it may seem that this tale is without hope, but God is like a master chess player. He knows every possible move we could make and has infinite wisdom for how He will handle whatever comes to pass. So God chose Noah, "a righteous man, blameless in his generations" (Genesis 6:9 ESV).

Noah was one of a kind in his day, and because he walked faithfully with God, he was chosen to redeem humanity from the flood. He was a foreshadower of the ultimate Redeemer, Jesus, who would one day come to rescue God's people and completely re-write God's Story.

Unfortunately, humanity's unholiness did not disappear with the receding waters of the flood, and sometime later, God began editing again.

This part of the story begins with one nation through which God decided to lay a framework and prepare the way for His ultimate redemption plan.

+ To read more about this bizarre Bible story, check out page 16 of the complimentary guide *Plan Your ESCAPE*. You can download it for FREE at HeatherRaeHutzel.com/PlanYourEscape

God started with a man named Abram, and through him and his bride, promised to bless the entire world. Abram was renamed Abraham as a marker of this promise, and he bore a son Isaac, who was the father of Jacob, who, with his descendants, became the nation of Israel. If you know anything about Israel, then you know, they too, had a bit of an enslavement problem and were in need of an escape.

The full story of the Israelite nation's enslavement and escape can be found in the book of Exodus, but here's a quick summary. Joseph, one of the sons of Jacob (Israel), came into favor with Pharaoh, the leader of Egypt, the most powerful nation in the ancient world. During a famine, Joseph's wisdom led him to be positioned as second in command only to Pharaoh. Due to their brother's service, Joseph's siblings and family would later come and find refuge in the country of Egypt. After many years, the death of Joseph, and a change in Egyptian rule, the Israelite nation was placed into forced slavery and in need of an escape. God heard their cries for help and raised up a leader, Moses, to deliver them from their slavery. In a sense, Moses became their freedom fighter.

The exodus from Egypt has become, in so many ways, an archetype for what it means to escape. Egypt, throughout the Bible, is always representative of "the world" or, as we've been calling it, the Story of the World. It symbolizes anything other than the perfect story in which God intended for us to live. Even Moses himself would come to represent Jesus Christ, our ultimate freedom fighter. The first celebration of the Passover paints a deep and meaningful picture of how Jesus redeemed us through His blood.

In the midst of the Israelites escape from slavery, Egypt fell prey to ten plagues, the final plague being the death of every firstborn son living in Egypt. God made it very clear that the Israelites, though they were "His people," were not exempt from this plague. Only by placing the blood of a lamb on the door posts of their homes would they be able to escape from the certain death of their firstborns.

The Israelite people were no stranger to the idea of animal sacrifice. It was something they and the surrounding nations had practiced for centuries. In fact, the sacrificial lamb was something that would deeply resonate with the Israelites. Many years earlier, their ancestral father Abraham was asked by God to sacrifice his son Isaac as a symbol of his devotion. As the story goes, God did not actually require Abraham to make the sacrifice. God didn't want to kill Abraham's son. He was trying to make a point.

Unfortunately, the idea of sacrificing His child would not have seemed entirely foreign to Abraham. Surrounding nations were accustomed to human sacrifice. Abraham would have also been familiar with the story of his ancestors, Adam and Eve in the garden. He knew God spared their lives and that there was an outstanding debt of death that would have to be paid.

So when Abraham took the wood for the burnt offering and placed it on his son Isaac to carry, He probably did not realize just how prophetic his words would become when Isaac asked a very important question. "Father? The fire and wood are here," Isaac said, "but where is the lamb for the burnt offering" (Genesis 22:7)?

Abraham answered him saying, "God himself will provide the lamb for the burnt offering, my son" (Genesis 22:8).

Of course, Abraham would have been distraught over this request from God. After all, God promised to make Abraham into a great nation through his son Isaac.

Ancient cultures did not have aspirations for individual success but rather success of the family. All hope for Abraham's family rested on the life of Isaac.

Hebrews 11 tells us that Abraham believed the words he spoke to his son. God would provide the lamb because God made a covenant with Abraham, promising to make his descendants as numerous as the sands on the seashore and the stars in the sky.

By faith Abraham, when God tested him, offered Isaac as a sacrifice. He who had embraced the promises was about to sacrifice his one and only son, even though God had said to him, "It is through Isaac that your offspring will be reckoned." Abraham reasoned that God could even raise the dead, and so in a manner of speaking he did receive Isaac back from death. (Hebrews 11:17-19)

Abraham came to the conclusion that if God required him to make the sacrifice, then He would also raise Isaac back to life again. Now that's faith! That's living a radical, set-apart life!

As we know, God didn't allow Abraham to kill his son. Through this test, Abraham's faithfulness was revealed and so was God's greater plan. God Himself would provide the lamb to fulfill the outstanding debt.

Returning to Egypt and the Passover story, we see God requiring very specific instructions for selecting and sacrificing the Passover lamb. Only a lamb or goat without spot or blemish could be used, a foreshadowing of what would be required in order to redeem us in our ultimate escape.

The night passed, and only those tucked safely away in a home that contained blood on the doorposts survived. In every house the next morning, there was either a dead child or a dead lamb. The message was clear. The lamb that was slain in order to protect each Israelite family was enough to shield them from the destroyer who entered the homes of the Egyptians, but it was not enough to save them from their impending death, ultimate separation from God.

The weight of their unholiness still clung to them. For one night they were spared, as Adam and Eve were spared when cast from the garden, yet they were not holy as God is holy. There was still a vast distance that would need to be crossed.

Now, I want to be very clear about something. Neither physical death nor spiritual death (separation from God) was ever a part of God's design for the world. God gave us free will because real love requires a choice. To revoke that free will would retract our ability to choose to love, which would, in turn, cancel our ability to bear His image. The creation of the entire universe hinges upon the fact that God made all created beings with the ability to choose Him or to not choose Him. But God's love for us is so great that He chose His own suffering over our suffering.

It's easy to forget God's loving plan in the midst of the Old Testament. The books of the Old Testament are some of the bloodiest and most gruesome pieces of recorded history. We have to remember, this was NOT God's desire. God knew if He didn't separate Himself from us, we would be immediately destroyed out of the natural consequences of our unholiness. God had a choice. He could either separate Himself from us for eternity or separate Himself for a period of time. God chose the latter and used that period of time to orchestrate a plan.

***

Shortly after their escape from Egypt, God gave the Israelite nation the foundation for what would become "The Law." The Ten Commandments were given to Moses at Mount Sinai, and a list of other laws and commands were bestowed throughout the Pentateuch, the first five books of the Bible. By the time Jesus arrived on the scene, the Jewish people were abiding by a list of 613 different laws.

The Jewish Law was a record of the commands God required of His people in order for them to make every effort to be holy as He is holy. The problem was they couldn't do it. It was impossible for the Israelite nation to keep each of the 613 laws, and those were only the ones God had given them. Many things considered sinful or immoral today weren't even mentioned, because God knew there was no possible way for us to be holy through our own actions and deeds.

God always meets us where we are because He knows how far we have fallen from His holy image that we once perfectly represented. God has to come to us because He knows we will never be able to make our way to Him.

Throughout history, humanity has attempted to make atonement for her own sins while God diligently loved, cared for, and guided His people toward the moment in time when He would redeem them. All along, humans believed there was only one way for us to be back in the presence of our God: to be holy as He is holy. It seemed hopeless that we could be reunited with Him, but we didn't realize there was another way to be one with God again. If we couldn't become holy as God is holy, then the only other option would be for God to become unholy as we are unholy. We could not make ourselves one with God, so He would have to make Himself one with us.

And thus our hero came to set us free. Jesus came for our escape.

**

He alone can bridge great chasms. Because of Him, dark voids, trenches, and distances too wide to cross are made passable.

In His name, a bridge of peace and healing is provided for the broken, gaping, wounded earth.

In Him, a way is made.

Because of Him, the path has been established. He bridges the unbridgeable. He connects the un-connectible. He carries old things across to the land of newness. He makes all things new. He makes a way in the desert and streams in the wasteland.

The great chasms of our broken hearts are crossed by Him alone. Our gaping wounds are made passable. The abyss of our soul is made penetrable. He makes a way across every trench, every valley, every canyon of misery and brokenness. His life and death is a bridge.

Our wandering hearts search to find something to bridge our great divide.

It is Him.

It has always, only, ever been Him.

Reconciliation comes when His name is whispered over the greatest gulfs. The syllables of His name become bricks and stones, paving the way to peace and healing and wholeness.

He is I Am.

He is the one who walks on water. He is the one who makes a way from death to life. No distance is too far. No trench unpassable. No chasm unconquerable. No broken valley of the shadow of death and despair un-traversable because of Him.

He makes the two, one.

He makes all things new.

He makes bridges out of our dust. He makes new passageways for us.

He is the way.

He is the life.

He is everything.

Jesus, He is our Great and Mighty Bridge.[+]

CHAPTER 7

HERO

[heer-oh]
noun

1. a man of distinguished courage or ability,
admired for his brave deeds and noble qualities:
*"The people believed there was no hope to be
rescued, but that's when the hero arrived."*

I once heard it said, "Our task is not to make
every Scripture mention Jesus, but to discover
how every text stands in relation to Him."

We need to realize that even though God had to
do some editing along the way, Jesus was not Plan
B in God's Story. He was Plan A. Jesus was a part
of God's plan and story all along.

Most Biblical scholars claim that Genesis 3:15 contains the very first prophecy of Jesus.

> I will put enmity
>   between you and the woman,
>   and between your offspring and hers;
> he will crush your head,
>   and you will strike his heel. (Genesis 3:15)

This verse is in the context of when God cursed the serpent after he tempted Adam and Eve. Now, while I agree this verse does foretell an impending savior, I would argue that the Bible reveals and foreshadows the coming of our hero much earlier in the story—in fact, from the very beginning of the story, from the very first documented words of God Himself. "And God said, 'Let there be light'" (Genesis 1:3).

The first recorded spoken words of the King reveal a prophecy and a proclamation of the coming Savior, Jesus Christ. Let me explain.

> In the beginning, God created the heavens and the earth. Now, the earth was formless and void, darkness was over the surface of the deep, and the Spirit of God was hovering over the waters. (Genesis 1:1-2)

If you are like me, you probably grew up imagining that these two verses describe a vast expanse of nothingness, a blank slate for God's creation, but let's take a closer look.

We talked a bit about Lucifer's rebellion, an event that a number of theologians suspect took place sometime before the events recorded in Genesis 1:1-2. We can even see references to the induction of this cosmic war in these two verses in Genesis, but in order to see it, we have to go back to the original language.

The original Hebrew for the words "formless and void" is "tohu bohu," which could also be translated as "to lie in waste, desolation, confusion, emptiness, chaos, indistinguishable ruin."[1] This doesn't sound like a blank slate. It sounds more like the aftermath of a war.

We see in the first two verses of the Bible that, yes, God did create the heavens and the earth, but something happened. Lucifer, along with a portion of the other heavenly hosts, revolted against God. At the point where we pick up the story, the universe, as we know it, is in a state of ruin.

Throughout the Bible, darkness is used as a way to represent evil and wickedness, which we see present in Genesis 1:2. And that part about God hovering over the waters? In ancient Near Eastern literature, "the sea" and "the deep" were terms used to describe the evil forces in the spiritual realm. Now when we take these things into consideration, the third verse of Genesis is so much more profound. Can't you picture it? God holding back the darkness and evil as He declares, "Let there be light!"

But it gets even better.

Take a look at the comparison below of Genesis

1. Strong's H8414 and H922, Blue Letter Bible. 5 May 2016. blueletterbible.org

1 and John 1. We will bounce back and forth between the two passages. The comparison is mind-blowing.

> Genesis: In the beginning, God created the heavens and the earth (Genesis 1:1).
>
> John: In the beginning was the Word, and the Word was with God, and the Word was God. He was with God in the beginning (John 1:1-2).
>
> Genesis: Now the earth was formless and empty, darkness was over the surface of the deep, and the Spirit of God was hovering over the waters (Genesis 1:2).
>
> John: Through him all things were made; without him nothing was made that has been made (John 1:3).
>
> Genesis: Then God said, "Let there be light." And there was light (Genesis 1:3).
>
> John: In him was life, and that life was the light of all mankind (John 1:4).
>
> Genesis: God saw that the light was good, and he separated the light from the darkness (Genesis 1:4).
>
> John: The light shines in the darkness, and the darkness has not overcome it (John 1:5).
>
> Genesis: God called the light, "day," and the darkness he called, "night" (Genesis 1:5).
>
> John: The true light that gives light to everyone was coming into the world (John 1:9).

Genesis: So God created mankind in his own image, in the image of God he created them; male and female he created them (Genesis 1:27).

John: The Word became flesh and made his dwelling among us. We have seen his glory (John 1:14).

Genesis: God saw all that he had made, and it was very good (Genesis 1:31).

John: No one has seen God at any time... he [Christ] has explained him (John 1:18 NASB).

Isn't that amazing?

Before human beings were even created, God was speaking light into our darkness. Before we needed a rescue plan, God was already providing one. From the dawn of all creation, God has been saying, "Let there be light!"

And what does light do? It illuminates. In the same way God created light that would illuminate and reveal His creation upon the earth, Jesus Christ illuminates and reveals God and His Story.

As we dive deeper into God's Story, we will see Jesus is not just the rescue plan to escape from our sin. He is the fulfillment of God's original story. He is our hero.

***

The Bible says Jesus is the Son of God, but "son of" means something very different in the Bible than what it means to us today. To us, "son of" means "the male child of so-and-so," but in the Bible, "son of" means "one who is like." This is a very important distinction to keep in mind when we are talking about Jesus.

Hebrews 1:3 says, "The Son is the radiance of God's glory and the exact representation of his being." Colossians 1:19 tells us, "God was pleased to have all his fullness dwell in him." And in John 5:18 it says, "[Jesus] was even calling God his own Father, making himself equal with God."

These verses tell us Jesus was not just the Son of God, as in the child of God, but the *exact* representation of God. He was God in the flesh. Jesus was fully God and fully man—God wrapped up in a human body. He *was* God.

Throughout history, Jesus was the only human being to live without sin because only God Himself is holy, spotless, and blameless. He was born of a woman and born of God. He lived a perfect life. He revealed to the world who God really is. He showed the world what it means to be holy as God is holy, and, maybe not so surprisingly, He revealed that the holiness of God is something so much deeper than we ever understood or imagined.

Unfortunately, the word "holy" has become synonymous with words like "righteous" and "moral," but it has a more profound meaning.

In chapter 6, we defined the word "holy" as meaning "set-apart," "different," and "other-worldly." This is the true meaning of the word.

The fact that God is sinless is one of the reasons why He is so different and set-apart. But more than that, God is radical, set-apart, and different by the nature of the love He has for us. There is nothing more holy than the all-encompassing, non-compromising, other-oriented love of the Almighty God. God's love for us is so great and so different that He specifically chooses to enter into situations with people that make Him appear unholy. Just look at Jesus. He hung out with prostitutes and drunkards. He went to parties. He touched lepers. He healed on the Sabbath. He spoke with women. To the outside world it appeared Jesus was breaking the law (being unholy), but the truth is this: what made Jesus so different and set-apart was that He was willing to get dirty. God is willing to take on our unholiness to be with us, and no place was this more clearly seen than the day Jesus hung on the cross.

On the cross, Jesus took on the appearance of a God-forsaken criminal. To the outside world, He looked like any other convicted sinner. He was mocked, beaten, bruised, scorned, and spat on. Curses were hurled at Him. He was convicted of crimes and wrongly accused. The one and only God, the only spotless, stainless Lamb, the only person that was holy as God was holy, was convicted of the very opposite thing. He was the only one worthy to enter into the presence of God. He was the only person who could stand before God and live, but He chose instead to take on our sins. He bore our iniquities in both a spiritual and physical sense (Isaiah 53:5).

As we saw before, sin is a deviation from Holiness. All have sinned and fallen short of the glory of God (Romans 3:23), that is, all except

Jesus. Because He took on our sin and unholiness, when Jesus died on earth, He became separate from Abba Father. (Death is separation from God.) Jesus experienced death in the same way we would, which is why He cried out, "Eloi, Eloi, lema sabachthani?" Which means, "My God, My God, why have you forsaken me" (Mark 15:34)?

Separation from God was the reason why Jesus came to earth. Jesus came with the intent of physically dying because then He could go to the one place where God was not—death.

Let us not forget that Jesus was God Himself. He was fully God and fully man, a man who had never sinned. He was holy, spotless, and blameless. Like a white rag absorbing a black stain, pure and holy Jesus absorbed our sin. He became unholy. He became our sin. Jesus, who in His very nature is God (and God is life) entered into death.

John 5:26 says, "For as the Father has life in himself, so he has granted the Son to have life in himself."

Therefore, Jesus carried life into death. And guess what happened? Death imploded! Death was swallowed up in life in the same way that darkness is devoured by light. Darkness cannot exist in light, and neither can death exist in the presence of life. Death has been swallowed up in victory (1 Corinthians 15:54)!

Though we were dead in our transgressions, because of his great love for us, God, who is rich in mercy, made us alive with Christ. It is by his grace that we have been saved. (Ephesians 2:4-5)

God went to the one place where He was not, the place where we were condemned because of our unholiness. Jesus went to the place called death and hell. He became our unholiness and sin in order that, once again, He might be made one with us. We could not make ourselves holy as God is holy, so God chose to become unholy as we are unholy.

The reason God is different and set-apart is because of His great love for us, a love that knows no boundaries. God revealed the ultimate holiness in the great distance He traversed in order to be one with us. The ultimate, all-holy act is becoming the very thing you are not in order to be with the ones you love most. Love is ascribing worth to another at cost to yourself, and there is no greater love than this, that a man lay down His life for a friend (John 15:13).

As if that weren't amazing enough, there is more.

Unholiness cannot exist in the presence of holiness, which is why God banished Adam and Eve from the Garden of Eden. So get this, when Jesus, God in the flesh, took on our sin, it was destroyed! God, in all His holiness, absorbed all of our unholiness. He became our sin in order to destroy it forever. Sin is gone! Our sins are forgiven. They have been made obsolete. Sin no longer exists.

Let me say that again.

Sin no longer exists!

Romans 8:1-4 puts it this way:

> There is now no condemnation for those who are in Christ Jesus, because through Christ Jesus the law of the Spirit who gives life has set you free from the law of sin and death. For what the law was powerless to do because it was weakened by the flesh, God did by sending his own Son in the likeness of sinful flesh to be a sin offering. And so he condemned sin in the flesh, in order that the righteous requirement of the law might be fully met in us, who do not live according to the flesh but according to the Spirit.

At the moment of Jesus' death, the world was shaken. Literally. Darkness fell over the land. The earth shook, rocks split, and tombs broke open. The bodies of many holy people who had died were raised to life. Even more incredibly, at the exact moment of Jesus' final breath, the curtain of the temple was torn in two from top to bottom (Matthew 27:50-52).

The curtain in the Jewish temple was significant. It was the dividing wall that separated the Holy of Holies (the place where God's presence dwelled) from humanity. The curtain signified the chasm that existed between God and humans. Only the priests who served in the temple were allowed to enter and only once a year. If they did not follow the strict guidelines laid out for them when it was their turn to enter behind the curtain, they were immediately struck dead.

But at the moment Jesus Christ, our God in the flesh, breathed His last breath, this curtain was torn. No small feat considering this curtain was likely close to sixty feet tall and several inches thick.

There was no longer a need to separate that space in the temple. There wasn't even a need to be separated from God anymore. The thing that alienated us from Him before was our unholiness, but now, God had taken on our unholiness. The Holy of Holies had become the Unholy of Unholies! God took on the epitome of our unholiness in order to be reunited with us and destroy our sin for good!

Our sin is destroyed, and the dividing wall between us and God has been demolished. BUT. This is only the case *if* we allow God to enter into our most unholy place. We need to personally allow God to become our sin (to become our unholiness) so He can destroy it with His holiness. The way for us to become one with God and reunite ourselves with Him for eternity is still the same—we must become holy as He is holy—but now it is actually possible. We have to allow His holiness to enter into us in the form of the Holy Spirit, who is Himself God. It will kill us, but it will also make us alive because death is swallowed up in victory!

We are dying to death and waking to life.

***

God's Story is not like a typical American Story. American stories have a beginning, middle, and end. God's Story falls more in line with Jewish literature. (Or rather, Jewish literature is modeled after God's Story.) In Jewish literature, you will not find the phrase, "And they lived happily ever after, the end," because in Jewish literature, there is no end. Instead, the pattern is this: beginning, middle, and new beginning.

When it comes to God's Story, there is no final chapter. God's Story is still being written, and even after Jesus returns, God's Story will not end. It will simply begin anew.

This is the story of God, not that someday all life will come to an end, but rather, through Jesus all death has come to an end. Our story began from the dust of the earth, but, praise God, it does not have to end the same way. Our story is God's Story, and God's Story doesn't end; it has only new beginnings.

This, dear reader, is God's Story, the story into which we were born. It is a radical love story about a crazy, unrelenting lover who is desperately seeking to reclaim and rescue His beloved. And rescue us He has!

Jesus Christ died for all men and women. By His death, Jesus freed all human beings throughout all eternity, in the time before He was born and after. Jesus died for everyone, even horrible people. Jesus died for Hitler. He died for the soldiers who nailed Him to the cross. He died for Judas, the disciple who betrayed Him. He died for the people who lived long before Him, like the enemies of His Jewish ancestors. He died for the people at the Tower of Babel and the people who died in the flood. He died for Adam and Eve. He died for me, and He died for you. We all have been set free.

When Jesus died on the cross, He unlocked the prison door of every human being who has ever lived throughout the history of the world. God didn't die just so you wouldn't suffer in hell. He died because He wants to be with you. He needs you! He wants to spend every second of every day with you. He is desperate for you. He is head over heels in love with you!

So does this mean no one goes to hell? God would like for it to be that way, but unfortunately, our prison cell has two locks, one on the outside and one on the inside. Jesus has already unlocked the outside of every cell in the prison. Have you unlocked your door from the inside? Have you thrown open the gates and allowed Jesus to come in with you?

Jesus has unlocked the outside of our prisons cells, and there He stands, tenderly knocking, praying you will open the door and let Him in.

Some people spend their whole lives locked inside their prison cell, all alone, never allowing Jesus to come in. This is what hell really is—a prison locked from the inside. People who don't open the door to God will die alone in their cell. God doesn't send people to hell. They choose to remain there. God gives us the desires of our hearts, even if that desire means we don't want to be with Him.

It is in those quiet moments, when we finally realize there is a God who loves us standing outside our door, that we see the true character of God. He is not holding out on us. He didn't banish us to this prison cell. We did. We willingly thrust our wrists before Satan, allowing him to bind us. God allowed us to go because He gave us free will. But because of His great love for us, since that day in the Garden of Eden, He has not stopped pursuing us. For thousands of years, God has orchestrated and rewritten His Story in order to put a rescue plan in place.

The prison is unlocked! The prisoners' shackles have been broken! But how many of us continue to remain trapped inside a lie we choose to believe?

Maybe you *have* opened the door. Maybe you've invited Jesus to step inside. Maybe you know Him intimately as the lover of your soul, yet you continue to live as a prisoner, the only difference being that Jesus now sits beside you as you clumsily pick at the locks on your chains. Perhaps now, for the first time in your life, you recognize that while you have accepted the freedom Jesus died to give you, you have never actually embraced that freedom.

Jesus loves us. He died for our freedom. But once we let Him in, dear Christian, His plan is not for us to remain inside our prison cells forever. Unfortunately, I have met far too many people who claim to be Christ-followers, who do nothing of the sort. If we are following Christ, it will require us to follow Him outside the prison door. Once we repent, we must believe. Once we escape, we must embrace our freedom. We have been set free! It's time to live as though it is true.

Let me remind you of what Paul so bluntly said in Galatians 5:1, "It is for freedom that Christ has set us free. Stand firm, then, and do not let yourselves be burdened again by a yoke of slavery."

I imagine Paul shouting this phrase to the people of the church of Galatia. I can almost see him face-palming as he shakes his head saying, "C'mon, guys. Jesus set you free so you would be free! Why are you still living like you are a slave?"

Is Jesus asking you the same thing? "Why are you living like a slave when I have died to set you free? Why do you sit here in this prison cell when the door is standing wide open? The Kingdom of God awaits you! There is a whole world outside you have never even seen. I can't wait to show you the amazingly wonderful story I have planned for your life."

Maybe this is all new for you. Maybe you have heard about God's Story before, but never like this. Maybe this all seems too good to be true: a loving God, a head-over-heels, crazy, in-love with you God who wants, no, NEEDS you! Since the moment He began writing His Story, you (Yes, you!), have been on God's mind. He is eagerly pursuing you. He is standing outside your prison door knocking. Knocking and praying. Praying and knocking.

"Open the door, Beloved. I have missed you for far too long. I have loved you with an everlasting love, and I don't want to live another second apart from you! Will you come? Will you follow me? Will you choose to live in a new story? Will you escape?"[+]

+ For discussion questions for this chapter, check out page 23 in the complimentary guide *Plan Your ESCAPE*. You can download it for FREE at HeatherRaeHutzel.com/PlanYourEscape

CHAPTER 8

THEME

[theem]
noun

1. a unifying or dominant idea, motif, etc., as in a
work of art:
*"While reading the story, a beautiful and surprising
theme began to emerge."*

W hew. What a story! And guess what? It
only gets better from here. Now, before we
dive into the next chapter of God's Story,
we need to hit the pause button for a minute and
talk about story structure.

Whether it's a book, a movie, or a bedtime fairy
tale, all good stories have a theme or a central point.

I like to think of it as a foundation upon which all the pieces of the story are built.

When God first began writing His Story and building His miraculous and marvelous Kingdom, He did what any good builder would do: He laid a foundation. Just as laying a strong and sturdy foundation would be at the top of your list if you were constructing a building, so too with God and the things He creates. Without a solid foundation, any structure, no matter how big or small, will struggle to stand. Jesus even uses this illustration to make a point in the parable about the wise and foolish builder. Jesus says in Matthew 7:24-27:

> Therefore everyone who hears these words of mine and puts them into practice is like a wise man who built his house on the rock. The rain came down, the streams rose, and the winds blew and beat against that house; yet it did not fall, because it had its foundation on the rock. But everyone who hears these words of mine and does not put them into practice is like a foolish man who built his house on sand. The rain came down, the streams rose, and the winds blew and beat against that house, and it fell with a great crash.

In the midst of a storm, the structures that have the highest chance of surviving are the ones that have the surest foundations. God knows this, so in creating His Story and Kingdom, one that was to be an eternal Kingdom without end, God needed to build the foundation on something of eternal caliber: Himself. 1 John 4:8 reveals to us who God is—God is love—so the theme of God's Story, the foundation upon which everything else is built, is love.

Love, by its very definition, requires that two or more parties be involved. So, in actuality, the foundation of God's Story is not just God's character of love but His love relationship with us. Imagine two interlocking slabs of durable stone. This is how we should picture the foundation of God's Story; it's the relationship between two key pieces: God's character and our identity.

We've already spent some time focusing on God as the main character of this story. God's true nature was revealed through the life of Jesus Christ. All of God's character and essence dwelled inside of Jesus. He was the exact representation of God. If we want to know what God is like, we need not look any further than Jesus.

But the foundation of God's Kingdom is built upon our relationship with Him, not just His character alone. In order to understand and grasp the theme of this story, we need to spend time talking about our identity as well.

Through the deception of the enemy, our foundational slab has been fragmented. The two pieces that were once pressed securely together have been broken apart. By implanting those two little lies, one about us and one about God, the enemy was able to create a domino effect that would eventually topple the entire structure of God's Story. In his mission, Satan succeeded in his attempt to corrupt, taint, and ultimately destroy the foundation so nothing could stand upon it. He swapped out our strong, solid foundation of being secure in our true identity and the true character of God with lies, insecurities, and a false picture of who God is. Through this, the enemy has convinced us that the true story is the one that is fiction.

Thankfully, while John 10:10 tells us that the thief, Satan, comes only to steal, kill, and destroy, Jesus came that we may have life, and have it to the full. Jesus didn't come just to deliver us from the bondage of sin that we might escape and be free. His purpose was not solely to reveal to us the true nature of God. No, there is another reason why Jesus came. When we examine His life in the context of the whole story, what Jesus did on the cross becomes even more amazing.

Satan may have told God the price to redeem us was too great, there was no amount He could pay to have us back, but God said, "How about Me? What if I give you Me instead?" In essence, the cross became God's way of slapping a price tag on us declaring, "You are worth all of Me!"

Something is only worth the price someone is willing to pay. So you see, the cross was not meant to simply be our get-out-of-jail-free card. No, the cross was God's way of redeeming our identity and establishing our worth.

It was God saying to us, "When I created you from the dust and dirt of the earth, I poured Myself out for you. I created you in My image. I made you to be a part of Me. In that moment, I established your worth. You are worth all of Me! And as I hang here on this cross, paying for you with My very life, once again, I establish your worth and your identity—all of Me."

Since the moment God first leaned forward and breathed life into His most prized creation, He has not once stopped pouring Himself out for us. God has been speaking out our identity since before the dawn of creation. We have always been His. That's what He came to show us on the cross. In the life of this one man, Jesus Christ of Nazareth, God made the boldest revelation in all of history. Stay with me because this is where it gets really good.

In his deception, Satan not only effectively destroyed our understanding of our identity but also our understanding of the character of God. Yet, God revealed to us His true nature and character through Jesus Christ on the cross. Jesus *was* God. He was the physical representation of the invisible God. We might even say He was "made in God's image." Sound familiar? Jesus not only revealed our identity by ascribing to us our worth, He not only exposed the truth of God's character, but He also perfectly represented what we as human beings were always meant to be from the dawn of our creation!

Do you understand what this means? Jesus came to restore our foundation. He came to reestablish what was broken in the Garden of Eden through the deception of the enemy. He came to reveal both the true character of God and the reality of our identity.

In the book of Isaiah it says, "See, I lay a stone in Zion, a tested stone, a precious cornerstone for a sure foundation" (Isaiah 28:16). In the Gospels, Jesus references Psalm 118 when talking about

Himself saying, "The stone the builders rejected has become the cornerstone" (Mark 12:10).

Jesus is the foundation upon which the Kingdom of God is built. He is the central theme of God's Story. He *is* the story, the Word of God. He reveals everything! He unveils God's truest intentions for humanity from the very beginning. He was the embodiment of the relationship between God and human beings. That's why it is so crucial for us to understand who Jesus is. This is why I am so blown away by the fact that I grew up in the church, yet I had no flipping clue who this man was!

Christ is our solid rock. These are not just some quaint words in a hymn; they are truth! Jesus fully embodied what it means to be God and what it means to be human. He is the key to everything. Everything hinges upon Jesus.

Before the fall, Adam and Eve were just like Jesus, and we were created to be like them. Hopefully, by now, you are starting to understand what I am saying. Sweet friend, please hear me when I say this: we were created to be just like Jesus, fully human and fully God's Spirit. *We are the Sons of God!*

Now, maybe this sounds blasphemous to you, but don't throw out this book just yet! The biggest obstacle we face when it comes to our escape is our lack of understanding when it comes to the reality of our identity. Our failure to comprehend is what hinders us more than anything else from living the radical, set-apart life we were called to live in God's Story. This, right here, this is *the* foundation.

Let me ask you a couple of questions. During His time on earth, who did Jesus claim to be? The Son of God. And for those who didn't follow Him, who did they think Jesus was? A blasphemer, a heretic, someone who operated under the power of demons. What Jesus said was crazy, absolutely nuts, but He rose from the grave! What He prophesied came true! He *was* the Son of God. And people all over the globe, even two-thousand years later, worship and follow and believe in the things He said and did.

Jesus was not what everyone expected. It's hard for us to imagine this now, but try to put yourself in the shoes of the Pharisees, the religious people of the day. They would be the equivalent of the church-goers, preachers, and ministers in our world. In their minds, they had a pre-conceived idea of who the Messiah would be. Unfortunately, because of the deception of the enemy, today we also have preconceived ideas of who we are and what the Church should be. But God's thoughts are not our thoughts. His ways are not our ways (Isaiah 55:8-9). They are higher and greater and better and crazier! They are radical and unexpected!

The Pharisees and teachers of the law were anticipating the Messiah, but they failed to understand what was right in front of them in the scriptures. (Let us not do the same thing today and miss what God is saying to us.) The Pharisees were anticipating a king, a mighty and militant leader, someone with stature and power who would lead them out from under the oppression of the Roman Empire. But what did they get?

Jesus: a carpenter from Nazareth, a bastard child, born out of wedlock. He grew up with them, played with their children, walked beside them on the roads, passed them in the fields, worshiped with them at the temple, and celebrated the feasts with them. As He grew older, He worked beside them, crafting objects for their homes. He bought from them at the markets. He taught them at the temple. He mourned with them. He sang with them. He dined with them and suffered under oppression with them. He seemed no different than anyone else.

The prophet Isaiah described Jesus this way:

He grew up before him like a tender shoot,
    and like a root out of dry ground.
He had no beauty or majesty to attract us to him,
    nothing in his appearance that we should desire him.
He was despised and rejected by mankind,
    a man of suffering, and familiar with pain.
Like one from whom people hide their faces
    he was despised, and we held him in low esteem. (Isaiah 53:2-3)

By earthly standards, there was nothing special about Jesus. They didn't realize who He was. They didn't understand that He *was* a king, the King of the Universe. He *was* a mighty, militant leader, the commanding officer of the Army of the Lord. He had more notoriety than anyone who ever lived, bearing the name of His Father in Heaven, a name so sacred that no one in His time would dare to speak it. He had the power of Heaven backing Him. All the authority in existence was at His fingertips, yet He revealed that the power of God is not like the power of the world. He even said to them,

> You know that those who are regarded as rulers of the Gentiles lord it over them, and their high officials exercise authority over them. Not so with you. Instead, whoever wants to become great among you must be your servant, and whoever wants to be first must be slave of all. For even the Son of Man did not come to be served, but to serve, and to give his life as a ransom for many. (Mark 10:42-45)

While the Pharisees were busy plotting His murder, they never considered Jesus would indeed be the one to lead them out from under their oppression, not from the Roman Empire, but their oppression from sin. He would be the one to lift the outstanding debt of death from their heads.

Jesus was not who the Pharisees said He was. He was who *He* said He was—the Son of God.

Let me say it bluntly. The entire Christian faith is founded on this one crazy concept—the God of the universe *became* a human being. In fact, if we dig deeper into the story of God, there are actually plenty of crazy concepts that Christ-followers claim to believe: talking donkeys, parting oceans, walking on water... Our God is a crazy God, and His Story is a crazy story! The Bible is not a nice, neat little collection of bedtime tales. It is a radical, dangerous, passionate, out-of-this-world epic saga! It is time for us to start living like the God we follow is not contained by the limitations of our physical world because clearly, He is not. He proved it when the infinite King of the universe chose to become finite and manifested Himself as a tiny embryo in the womb of a peasant virgin. So please don't tell me what I am saying is too crazy. Our God *is* too crazy. If we follow Him, crazy should be our norm!

So let me say it again, and this time consider that, just maybe, our crazy and amazing God wants you to understand the crazy and amazing identity He has bestowed upon us. *We are the Sons of God.*

"What is a Son of God?" you ask. It is one human life that is completely and whole-heartedly sold-out to the Spirit of God who lives inside of them.

"Son of God" is a title; it was the title given to Jesus Christ and now it is given to us. It means more than "we are God's children;" it means we bear His image and His name. It means His inheritance belongs to us. The term "Son of God" has nothing to do with gender and everything to do with authority and power. It is not the same to say that we are "sons and daughters" of our God, because in ancient Near Eastern families, daughters did not hold the same rights as sons. The son of a father was given wealth and inheritance. *Everything* the father owned belonged to the son, including the father's power and authority. The son was able to stand in during the father's absence. The son represented the father and everything he was about. The son's aspirations were to honor the father and carry out the father's work. This is why I make this very important distinction in calling us "Sons of God," not "sons and daughters." To be called the Son of God is to be given the most honorable title in the heavenly realm, second only to the Most High.

So let me ask the question again: "What is a Son of God?" It is a person (male or female) who, like Jesus, reflects God's character of unrelenting love because He has given us His authority and power. It is a person who never waivers from reflecting God's image and carrying out His work, even if it means being obedient to death, even death on a cross (Philippians 2:8).

Before we can be the church, we have to understand that our identity is inextricably tied to the character of God as seen in Jesus. When our identity as a Son of God is solidified, that is when we identify with our mission—the will of the Father. When we are secure in our identity, our hearts bleed for the things that His does. Our eyes see what His see, our feet go where His go, and our hands do what His do. We will not have to *try* to be the Church; we will simply *be* the Church.

***

On this side of the cross, God is offering us the same gift He offered Adam and Eve: deep, intimate, interlocking relationship with Him. In the same way that God placed Himself inside Adam and Eve, He placed Himself inside Jesus, and that's what He wants to do with us. He wants to give us the Holy Spirit.

This means, in the same way that Jesus Christ was a physical body God dwelt in, we too are physical bodies God dwells in. Jesus reveals what our identity is: the temple of the Holy Spirit, the dwelling place of God.

Unfortunately, some of the phrases we use when talking about God have become too familiar. Familiarity is one of our biggest hindrances to understanding God. That's why we're still stuck inside these prison cells. They have become familiar to us. The deception we believe seems normal. Put aside everything you know about God for a moment. Read these words and see them as if it were the first time.

Okay, here we go.

If you have the Holy Spirit inside you, then you have God inside you.

GOD IS INSIDE YOU.

God lives in you. You are the temple of the Holy God of the universe. Your body is where He hangs out.

Think about it. God—the creator of the heavens and the earth, the one who parted the Red Sea, the one who walked on water, the one who conquered death, is living inside of us! If this is true, quite frankly I can't understand why we all aren't falling out of bed every morning screaming, "The Almighty God is freaking living inside my body!"

We are one with God in the *exact same way* Jesus Christ was one with God!

Jesus puts it this way in the Gospel of John:

If you love me, keep my commands. And I will ask the Father, and he will give you another advocate to help you and be with you forever—the Spirit of truth. The world cannot accept him, because it neither sees him nor knows him. But you know him, for he lives with you and will be in you. I will not leave you as orphans; I will come to you. Before long, the world will not see me anymore, but you will see me. Because I live, you also will live. On that day you will realize that I am in my Father, and you are in me, and I am in you. Whoever has my commands and keeps them is the one who loves me. The one who loves me will be loved by my Father, and I too will love them and show myself to them. (John 14:15-21)

And in John chapter 17 Jesus said:

My prayer is not for them alone. I pray also for those who will believe in me through their message, that all of them may be one, Father, just as you are in me and I am in you. May they also be in us so that the world may believe that you have sent me. I have given them the glory that you gave me, that they may be one as we are one—I in them and you in me—so that they may be brought to complete unity. Then the world will know that you sent me and have loved them even as you have loved me.

Father, I want those you have given me to be with me where I am, and to see my glory, the glory you have given me because you loved me before the creation of the world.

Righteous Father, though the world does not know you, I know you, and they know that you have sent me. I have made you known to them, and will continue to make you known in order that the love you have for me may be in them and that I myself may be in them. (John 17:20-26)

Our identity is the holy temple of God. We, like Jesus, are literally a physical body God dwells in. We are the Sons of God!

See what great love the Father has lavished on us, that we should be called children of God! And that is what we are! The reason the world does not know us is that it did not know him. Dear friends, now we are children of God, and what we will be has not yet been made known. But we know that when Christ appears, *we shall be like him,* for we shall see him as he is. All who have this hope in him purify themselves, just as he is pure. (1 John 3:1-3, emphasis mine.)

This is what God had in mind the whole time. From the moment of our inception, God's love has been towards us. He desired us. He needed us, and He was willing to do ANYTHING to have us back.

God longs for us to say "anything" to Him because He was willing to say "anything" to us.

This is ridiculously good news, but perhaps you are overwhelmed by it and wondering, "Where do I go from here?" Well, I think 1 Corinthians 6:19-20 says it best.

> Do you not know that your bodies are temples of the Holy Spirit, who is in you, whom you have received from God? You are not your own; you were bought at a price [a very great and precious price]. Therefore honor God with your bodies.

How do we honor Him with our bodies? We live as Jesus did. Our purpose in life is to tell the story of God. With the song of our lives, we are to reflect the theme of this miraculous tale: Jesus.

"If anyone obeys his word, love for God is truly made complete in them. This is how we know we are in him: Whoever claims to live in him must live as Jesus did" (1 John 2:5-6).

Here's the best part. We *can* live as Jesus did. The power of Jesus we see illustrated in the Gospels also resides in us because we have the exact same Spirit in us.[+] In fact, Jesus Himself went on to say that we, meaning the church, will do even greater things than Jesus did. Now, you might be wondering, "How is that even possible? How could we be greater than Jesus?"

It's simple. It's because there was only one of

+ Read more about the power God bestows on us on page 24 of the complimentary guide *Plan Your ESCAPE*. You can download it for FREE at HeatherRaeHutzel.com/PlanYourEscape

Him, and there are millions of us!

This is what it means to be the Church, the body of Christ! This is what it means to be human, created in the image of God. We are to be like Jesus, a reflection of God to a lost and dying world. The world has forgotten the story of God, and they have forgotten what God looks like—LOVE! But not just any kind of love, a God-like kind of love, a Jesus-like kind of love, the kind of love that is not only the verb that God does but also the noun that He is!

"And this is how we know what love is, Jesus Christ laid down his life for us. And we ought to lay down our lives for one another" (1 John 3:16).

We are to be a people who love recklessly and sacrificially. We are to love with abandon because that is how God loves us, and He lives inside of us. God wants us to contain what we were always meant to contain—Him! We were made to be His temple.

***

Each and every one of us who bears the image of God and His Spirit within us is like a chiseled piece of marble, a foundational stone, hand-carved by God, made for a noble purpose.

God wants every piece, every brick, every stone of His temple to look exactly like the cornerstone, the foundation, Jesus. We all need to be stones of this caliber because it is only when we are together that we form God's temple, a strong and sturdy shelter for the lost, the last, and the least.

Ephesians 2:19-22 says we are:

> ...members of his household, built on the foundation of the apostles and prophets, with Christ Jesus himself as the chief cornerstone. In him the whole building is joined together and rises to become a holy temple in the Lord. And in him you too are being built together to become a dwelling in which God lives by his Spirit.

There is a problem though. There is something that hinders us from achieving the ideal God has for us. The stones for the temple are scattered across the earth like a pile of rubble strewn about a desert floor. We the church are not united. We are living a lie, a work of fiction. We have settled for a life of mediocrity. We are living far beneath the level of greatness for which we have been called.

Take a look at what 1 Peter 2 says:

> As you come to him, the living Stone—rejected by humans but chosen by God and precious to him—you also, like living stones, are being built into a spiritual house to be a holy priesthood, offering spiritual sacrifices acceptable to God through Jesus Christ. For in Scripture it says:
>
> "See, I lay a stone in Zion,
>   a chosen and precious cornerstone,
> and the one who trusts in him

will never be put to shame."
Now to you who believe, this stone is precious. But to those who do not believe,

"The stone the builders rejected
has become the cornerstone,"
and,

"A stone that causes people to stumble
and a rock that makes them fall."
They stumble because they disobey the message—which is also what they were destined for. (1 Peter 2:4-8)

Don't let Jesus become a stumbling block to you. Let Him be your cornerstone, your foundation, the perfect example of who God created you to be. Why? Because:

...you are a chosen people, a royal priesthood, a holy nation, God's special possession, that you may declare the praises of him who called you out of darkness into his wonderful light. Once you were not a people, but now you are the people of God; once you had not received mercy, but now you have received mercy. (1 Peter 2:9-10)

Now please know this, we are NOT God. We don't become God. It is more beautiful than that. Our individuality and identity is retained. It must be retained; otherwise, there is no relationship. We become a part of Him, yet remain separate as well.

We overlap at our centers, abiding and remaining in God as He abides and remains in us. We become a piece of Him, an extension of who He is—love. It is far more beautiful than if we were to become Him. We remain who were are, but we take on His nature, and He remains who He is, but He takes on our nature. We become intertwined at our Spirits. We get tangled up in Him, and He gets tangled up in us. The goal is that we wouldn't be able to tell where one ends and the other begins.

Sweet friend, you and I, we were created to be a chosen people, a royal priesthood, a holy nation, the Sons of God. Free people living as free people. A people who have escaped.

Romans 8:14-17 says it this way:

> Those who are led by the Spirit of God are the children of God. The Spirit you received does not make you slaves, so that you live in fear again; rather, the Spirit you received brought about your adoption to sonship. And by him we cry, "Abba, Father." The Spirit himself testifies with our spirit that we are God's children. Now if we are children, then we are heirs—heirs of God and co-heirs with Christ, if indeed we share in his sufferings in order that we may also share in his glory.

I know what you're thinking. "This sounds too good to be true. How can this be possible?"

I know. I've thought the same thing, but let's be honest: these words resonate with us. There is a stirring deep within us, an unsettling voice that cries out from the depths of our souls saying, "We were made for more!" We all hear that voice. It's the voice of the story's main character calling us to step up and participate.

We are in the final chapter of God's Story. We have a role to play. We *are* made for more. It's time that we as the Church body unite.

We need to rise up from the ashes, emerge from the rubble, pick up the pieces, and carry them back to the cornerstone, the foundation. It's time to rebuild the temple.[+]

[+] For discussion questions for this chapter, check out page 27 in the complimentary guide *Plan Your ESCAPE*. You can download it for FREE at HeatherRaeHutzel.com/PlanYourEscape

CHAPTER 9

OLD

[ohld]
noun

1. former time, often time long past
"Feeling no regrets, he turned and left behind his old life."

We've reached the turning point in our journey. You now know everything you need in order to make the biggest decision of your life. Whether you have attended church for years or have never set foot inside the doors of a sanctuary. Whether you have known Jesus since you were a child or for the first time are hearing about Him and the sacrifice He made for you. Regardless of who you are or where you come from, right now, you have reached a crossroads. It's time to make a decision. *"In which story will you choose to live?"*

Imagine for a moment you are walking down a long and desolate road. Hear the gravel crunch softly under your feet as you stroll down the path. Feel the breeze on your cheeks. Let the scene become real to you. Let the visual of this moment imprint forever on your mind.

Keep your eyes fixed straight ahead as you continue walking. There's no need to look back. You won't be returning.

Do you see that tree up ahead in the distance? Yeah, that's the one. Go ahead and keeping walking until you reach the tree. That's where the road ends. Are you there? Great.

Allow the silence to envelope you as you take in the scene. Here before you, the road splits in two. Take in the vast differences in the two trails and their striking contrast to the road you were previously traveling. The road you are currently standing on ends here. There is no continuation of this current path on either of the two directions up ahead. They are distinct from one another and from the road you have been traveling. Two new journeys lay ahead.

The road you were traveling up until now represents your life, and this chapter is your arrival at the crossroads.

At some point in our lives, we are all faced with a situation of great magnitude. A circumstance in life that calls us to make a decision, and no matter which option we choose, it will alter the course of our lives forever. The very fact you are reading these words indicates you are about to face one of these moments. You have reached the fork in the road.

I must give you fair warning, however. Consider these words to be the yellow caution sign looming ominously before you. This is the sign planted firmly between both paths, the sign that reads "No Outlet. No Turning Back."

There are only two choices that lie at the end of this chapter, and you will be required to make a decision. No matter which one you choose, there is no turning back. You will be forced to declare which road you will travel and in which story you will live. You must decide where your allegiance lies.

When it comes to the story of God, you are either "for" or "against," "hot" or "cold." There is no "middle ground." There is no "lukewarm." You cannot read the words of this book, understand them at a core level, and declare neutrality. You cannot remain at the crossroads. You are either all in or all out.

In any great story, the heroic character is always faced with one of these pivotal decisions. It's the moment the hero understands the stakes of the journey and must choose whether or not to continue on the adventure. Perhaps the most iconic movie scene depicting the magnitude of such a decision comes from the movie *The Matrix*.

The ominous scene is set in a dimly lit room. Outside, thunder bellows and rain pelts the windows. A very solemn Morpheus invites the main character Neo to have a seat. Dressed in all black, his eyes hidden behind dark sunglasses, Morpheus appears almost sinister. His intentions are uncertain. One thing is clear, though: whatever he is about to say is important.

Morpheus asks Neo the question of a lifetime, "Do you want to know what the Matrix is?"

Neo nods.

"The Matrix is everywhere," Morpheus tells him. "It is all around us, even now in this very room. You can see it when you look out your window or when you turn on your television." His slow and deliberate voice continues. "You can feel it when you go to work, when you go to church, when you pay your taxes. It is the world that has been pulled over your eyes to blind you from the truth."

"What truth?" Neo whispers.

"That you are a slave, Neo." Thunder punctuates his words. "Like everyone else, you were born into bondage. Born into a prison that you cannot smell or taste or touch. A prison for your mind. Unfortunately, no one can be told what the Matrix is."

Morpheus opens a small box and empties its contents into the palm of his hand. "You have to see it for yourself."

Morpheus extends his hand and reveals two small objects—a red pill and a blue pill.

"This is your last chance," Morpheus warns Neo. "After this, there is no turning back. You take the blue pill, the story ends. You wake up in your bed and believe whatever you want to believe." He pauses. "You take the red pill, you stay in Wonderland, and I show you how deep the rabbit hole goes."

Neo begins to reach for the pills, but Morpheus interjects. "Remember," thunder crackles, "all I'm offering is the truth. Nothing more."

Friend, the world we live in is not so unlike the fantasy world of *The Matrix*. This movie is actually scary-accurate when it comes to depicting the Story of the World.

The Story of the World is everywhere. It is all around you, even now wherever you are reading this book. You can see it when you look out your window or when you turn on your television. You can feel it when you go to work, when you go to church, or when you pay your taxes. It is the world that has been pulled over your eyes to blind you from the truth. What truth? That you are a slave. Like everyone else, you were born into bondage. Born into a prison that you cannot smell or taste or touch. A prison for your mind. Unfortunately, no one can be told what the Story of the World is. You have to see it for yourself.

This is your last chance. After this, there is no turning back. You close the book here, the story ends. You go on living your life and believe whatever you want to believe. But if you turn the page, if you continue reading, I'll show you just how deep the rabbit hole goes.

Remember, all I'm offering is the truth. Nothing more.

Therefore, as your "Spiritual Morpheus," I beg the question, "Which path will you choose?"

In Jeremiah 6:16, the Lord says, "Stand at the crossroads and look; ask for the ancient paths, ask where the good way is, and walk in it, and you will find rest for your souls." But do you know what the very next line of that verse says? It reads, "But you said, 'We will not walk in it.'"

I pray that by the end of this chapter, you will boldly stand beside me, taking a brave step forward declaring, "No, I *will* walk in it."

***

I've found that many of us, who claim to be Christ-followers, are often spiritually educated beyond our level of obedience. When it comes to the Kingdom of God, it's not "the more we know, the better;" it's "the more we follow, the better." Let me explain.

There are many different terms used in our culture today to describe God's people: Christians, believers, followers, and disciples. But let's set the record straight. Unless we follow, we are *not* followers.

Here on earth, we are called to live in the original story God planned for us, fulfilling our original role. The Bible tells us Jesus came to be our perfect example of what we as humans were always meant to be: God's image bearers. He did this by doing and saying what His Father commanded Him to do. Jesus was a follower of His Father in Heaven.

In the Gospel of John, Jesus said, "I do nothing on my own but say only what the Father has taught me" (John 8:28 NLT). Jesus followed God

124

perfectly, and that is what we are to strive towards when we choose to live in God's Story. In verse 31 of the same chapter, Jesus continues by saying, "You are truly my disciples if you remain faithful to my teachings."

If we, like Jesus, are a Son of God, then our Father expects our obedience. We are to be His ambassadors, His reflection to the world. Remember when I said, "Of all the parts of my story, it always sounds the strangest when I say, 'I grew up in the church, but I didn't meet Jesus until I was in my twenties?'" If we, the Church, are not Jesus to the world, then who will be? It is the Church who is called to look like Him and be like Him in every way. We do this by doing what Jesus did: we follow.

Here's the challenging part: the more we know and believe about God, the more He expects from us. If God tells you to change something about the way you live your life, as His son, He expects you to follow through and obey, just as Jesus did. This is how we show our love to God.

Jesus said in John 14:24, "Anyone who does not love me will not obey my teaching. These words you hear are not my own; they belong to the Father who sent me."

Many times obeying costs us something. It certainly did for Jesus who, "being found in appearance as a man, humbled Himself by becoming obedient to death—even death on a cross" (Philippians 2:8).

Following God and living in His Story is not easy. I apologize if you have been told you can invite Jesus into your heart, and then everything will be just peachy. Unfortunately, the church has convoluted God's Story. As Søren Kierkegaard once said, "The matter is quite simple. The Bible is very easy to understand. But we Christians are a bunch of scheming swindlers. We pretend to be unable to understand it because we know very well that the minute we understand, we are obliged to act accordingly."[1]

We've turned the gospel into something that is difficult to understand and easy to carry out: just pray a prayer, just raise your hand, just walk an aisle, just dunk yourself in some water... The truth is the gospel is easy to understand but super hard to do. Here's the gospel in a nutshell: God is love, and we are to be a reflection of God. As Mother Teresa used to say, "Love until it hurts, and then love more." Simple to understand, hard to carry out, but oh so worth it!

What does it mean to be a reflection of God to the world?[+] It means ascribing worth to everyone we meet, even if it costs us something. That "something" might be time, money, our reputation, our resources, our patience, or perhaps, even someday, our lives. Becoming a follower of God requires us to give up everything, or at least, be ready and willing to if He should ask. It means saying "yes" to God, following when He says "come," staying when He says "stay." It's saying

---

1. Kierkegaard, Søren. *Provocations: Spiritual writings of Kierkegaard*, ed. Charles E. Moore. Farmington, PA: Plough, 2002.

+ You can read more about reflecting God's image on page 28 of the complimentary guide *Plan Your ESCAPE*. You can download it for FREE at HeatherRaeHutzel.com/PlanYourEscape

"anything" to Him because He said "anything" to us. It's making a bold declaration with our lives, a commitment to make all of us look like all of Him. It's already true in your Spirit, but will you make it true with your life? Will you live in the story for which you have been created? Or will you choose to live a lie, a work of fiction? It's a conscious choice we have to make.

You now know enough to make this decision, but I am cautioning you: you are also now accountable for this decision. Following God is not a spectator sport. It requires our whole selves. If you choose to follow Jesus and escape the Story of the World, you will be held accountable for everything He places before you now and in the future. If you want to escape fully from your prison of sin, deception, addiction, fiction, shame, religion, greed, passivity… whatever it might be, you need to be willing to follow your Redeemer to the ends of the earth and beyond. Only He knows where your freedom lies, and He wants to take you to that land—the Kingdom of God.

The Kingdom of God is here and now. We can live as God's Holy people now! In fact, that's what He wants for us. God doesn't want us to wait until we die to start living as His people in His Kingdom. He wants this to be our reality today.

When you escape and choose the way of Jesus, you die to yourself here and now. You die to your old way of life. This is what baptism symbolizes: death and resurrection, just like Jesus experienced. If a person gets baptized, their life should look profoundly different than before they made that choice, and I'm not just talking about removing sin from their life. When we choose to be baptized, it is just the beginning because dying is just the beginning. Dying is the thing that must happen before we can be raised from the dead; it is the moment before new life begins. If we want to be resurrected, we first have to die.

Not only do we need to allow God to put to death everything in our life that doesn't look like Him (sin), but we must also allow Him to bring to life new things that do look like Him. When we choose to escape our old way of life and embrace a new life in a new story, by the re-creative power of our God, we literally become a new creation. The apostle Paul says it best in 2 Corinthians 5:15-21:

> And he died for all, that those who live should no longer live for themselves but for him who died for them and was raised again. So from now on we regard no one from a worldly point of view. Though we once regarded Christ in this way, we do so no longer. Therefore, if anyone is in Christ, the new creation has come: the old has gone, the new is here! All this is from God, who reconciled us to himself through Christ and gave us the ministry of reconciliation: that God was reconciling the world to himself in Christ, not counting people's sins against them. And he has committed to us the message of reconciliation. We are therefore Christ's ambassadors, as though God were making his appeal through us. We implore

you on Christ's behalf: Be reconciled to God. God made him who had no sin to be sin for us, so that in him we might become the righteousness of God.

As Paul said, I implore you, sweet friend, be reconciled to God! Whatever it looks like for you, make the decision today to escape. Regardless of where you are in your relationship with God, whether you have known Him for years or are meeting Him for the very first time, you have an opportunity to take the next bold step in your journey. You have a choice to turn the page. You decide whether or not to move on to the next chapter. Only you can make this decision.

As you contemplate your next move, I'd like to leave you with the words of Spanish explorer Captain Hernán Cortés. In 1519, Cortés and his team of 600 men landed on the shores of Veracruz, Mexico. With intentions of conquering the Aztec Empire and colonizing a new kingdom, Cortés gave the bold, radical, and perhaps crazy order for his men to "burn the ships" that they not return.

God is asking you and me to do the same thing. This is what it means to repent. The word repent in Greek is metanoéō, which means to turn away or do differently. To repent is to turn 180 degrees, to do an about-face. It's to die to your old way of life, to put it to death. Completely. Paul said it this way in Philippians 3:13-14, "Forgetting what is behind and straining toward what is ahead, I press on toward the goal to win the prize for which God has called me heavenward in Christ Jesus."

In other words, *burn your ships*. Burn your prison cell. Burn your old story. Leave nothing left of your old way of life. You don't need it anymore. You're not coming back. It's time to escape and embrace a new life, a new story, and a new identity as God's chosen and holy people, a people who were made for more![+]

[+] For discussion questions for this chapter, check out page 30 in the complimentary guide *Plan Your ESCAPE*. You can download it for FREE at HeatherRaeHutzel.com/PlanYourEscape

INTERLUDE

[in-ter-lood]
noun

1. a period of time or different activity between
longer periods, processes, or events:
*"The interlude provided space to reflect and
process before the story continued."*

I f you are reading these words, I want to take a
moment to pause and celebrate. Hooray! You've
turned the page, burned your ships, and left your
prison cell! You've made the decision to escape and
have entered a new chapter in God's Story.

But let me also pause here to ask you a question.
Why? Why did you choose to escape?

I think I know why. I believe you made this
decision based on the very same reason I did—
Jesus. You didn't make this decision because of

fear. You weren't threatened with hell or eternal damnation. No. You discovered the truth of God's Story.

As Romans 2:4 says, it was God's kindness that led you to repentance. Through the power of God's Story, you discovered the truth of who God really is—Love—and the reality of your identity—you were made for more. You've experienced a renewal in your spirit. Jesus has become real to you, and now you can make Him real to others.

Cling to this renewal, dear reader. This is just the beginning. The journey starts here. You've changed your story, and through this, your life will be forever transformed. You will live the life of "more" for which God destined you as a member of the body of Christ, the people group who will revolutionize the world!

We will never see the Church's potential fulfilled without remembering God's Story, because it is through this story that we renew our understanding of God's character and our identity. It is only when the God we follow, the cornerstone upon which we build our lives, looks like Jesus on the cross that we can come together and rebuild the temple–God's Church.

What God says of us is true—we *were* made for more. It's time to believe it. It's time to embrace it. It's time to revive hearts and souls for the Kingdom of God. We need to release and empower the Church to be who she was always made to be—the Bride of Christ. When we embrace and believe this truth, when it really sinks in that we were made for a radical, set-apart life, nothing will be able to stop us. We will be able to do *anything*!

We are the Church. We are the revolution. We are going to change the world.

The Kingdom of God is at hand, sweet friend. It's time to embrace it!

PART II

EMBRACE
(BELIEVE)

CHAPTER 10

RADICAL

[rad-i-kuh l]
adjective

1. thoroughgoing or extreme, especially as regards change from accepted or traditional forms: *"The character's courage and zeal propelled his radical lifestyle."*

Imagine yourself standing at the threshold of the unknown, the place where the earth fades away and disappears into a sea of endless blue. Feel the cool water as it laps at the shore and rolls over your bare toes. Hear a voice call to you from somewhere beyond the deep, beckoning you forward out into the water.

"Come."

You hesitate, not knowing what lies ahead. The horizon stretches wide and uninterrupted. Not a single piece of land punctuates the view. Whitecaps roll in the distance, and waves beat heavy against the shore, mimicking the rhythm of your heart in your chest.

"Come."

Cautiously, you step forward. Your foot disappears beneath the water as the sea kisses your ankles.

"Come."

Your lower legs are buried as a wave threatens to overpower you. Your feet fail, and you lose your footing. Another wave barrels into you, but just before you fall, you hear a calming voice steady you.

"Come."

Dark clouds form an ominous line above the horizon where sea and sky collide. A rumbling in the distance warns you to come no further. The waters encircle your knees.

"Come."

A flash of light. A blustery gale. A shiver travels up your spine as the cold, dark liquid swallows your legs.

"Come."

Your waist drops into the abyss as the waves swell. You wipe the spray from your eyes and brace yourself against the storm.

"Come."

More thunder. More lightning. You should turn back now. It's not safe.

"Come."

You can no longer see the shore. Night has descended with the storm. The winds howl against the waves, screaming at you to turn back.

"Come."

You're up to your chest in icy water. Your breathing is labored as the cold presses in and suffocates. Your foot slips, but you catch yourself just in time, keeping your chin above the waves.

"Come."

You brace yourself against the storm. Your lips beneath the water, your nose above, you've reached the end. You've gone as far as you can. The storm threatens to drown you. The waves mock your attempts. You want to turn back.

"Come."

Silence. You wait.

"Come."

You hesitate.

"Come."

Thunder. Lightning. Waves and storm.

A gentle voice. A tender whisper. An unspoken promise.

"Come."

Ahead, the ocean swells. A wall of water forms. It rises, stretches, towering over you with a menacing growl.

"Come."

Without even pausing for a final breath, you step forward. The ground falls away. Your head slips beneath the surface as you fall. Your body is enveloped in the darkness, but as you sink below, warmth spreads over you. You're swept down and up. The tower of water collapses above you, but below, you are rocked by the embrace of the sea. You're wrapped in the warmth of the ocean. The surf above crashes violently, but you sway. You roll. You dance. You fly.

You tumble downward. You're swept upward.

You are consumed.

You breathe in, giving everything. Giving every piece of you. Holding nothing back. Not even your life. All is given. All is here. You are His.

***

Now that you have escaped, the question you have to ask yourself is, "What does it look like to embrace the freedom you have been given? What does it look like to embrace a radical, set-apart life in God's Story?"

Well, oftentimes, it looks a little crazy. A life lived in God's Story is radical and so very different from our old way of life.

The world's story tries to tell us who we are and what our purpose is, but God's Story says something different. God tells us our old self has died, and now, we are made for something more. This is truth. Believing or embracing this fact is a matter of living and acting according to the truth.

We are living in a different narrative now, and in order to fulfill our purpose and role, we must submit to the new story and the Author who is writing it. Jesus is the Lord of our life. He is the Author of this story, and so we yield to Him and the radical, set-apart life He has for us.

God does have a life of "more" He wants to give us, but we will never experience this "more" if we don't accept it when God offers it.

"Easy," you say. "I'm ready to accept all the exciting things God has for me!"

Well, not so fast.

Here's the thing about the radical, set-apart life God has for us—it is radical, and it is set-apart.

If you remember, this is the very definition of the word "holy." To be holy is to be set-apart. 1 Peter 1:14-16 says it this way:

> As obedient children, do not conform to the evil desires you had when you lived in ignorance. But just as he who called you is holy, so be holy in all you do; for it is written: "Be holy, because I am holy."

We are called to be holy as God is holy because He made us holy. God has set us apart as His chosen people, a royal priesthood, a holy nation, His own special possession. Therefore, we must live like it is true.

We must never forget, though, that what God says is holy and set-apart often looks very different from what we, the world, or even our churches may think.

In the time when Jesus lived, the Pharisees were the religious leaders of the day. They too placed a high importance on "living set-apart" and "being holy." They did this by separating themselves from the things (and people) that were considered unclean, things that were dirty and unholy according to the law. This is how the Pharisees attempted to make themselves holy, but as we've seen, Jesus modeled holiness in a very different way.

For Jesus, holiness was the process of walking into our mess; it was going to the unclean people and things that were traditionally unholy. God brought His holiness to us that we may be holy. Therefore, we are not to separate ourselves from the culture and from the things that may seem unholy, but rather, like Jesus, we are to bring our holiness into those dark places and carry light into the darkness. There is nothing more holy and set-apart than the radical love of God, and we are to be holy as He is holy, set-apart as He is set-apart, and radical as He is radical. As Ephesians 4:1 says, we must "live a life worthy of the calling we have received," and that is to "love because He first loved us" (1 John 4:19). It may seem crazy, it may seem radical, but that is the nature of our God.

Oftentimes, when we first start following God, He calls us to something crazy, or at least, it seems crazy in comparison to our old story and old way of life. It feels counterintuitive, and yes, very set-apart. But following God means following anywhere, even if it means venturing out into the waters of a stormy sea.

The Bible is loaded with stories of individuals who took a radical step of faith to follow God. That's why these stories are in the Bible. The people in the Bible were used by God not because they were uniquely suited for a task, but because they were uniquely brave. You don't earn yourself a page in God's Story by living a safe, comfortable life. Rather, our lives become sentences amidst God's greater story when we are willing to boldly obey and follow Him, even to the ends of the earth.

Think about the disciple Peter, who, in a moment of sheer courage (or perhaps insanity), stepped out of the boat where the other disciples remained in order to walk upon the stormy waves with Jesus. That took guts. Or what about the Israelite nation who set aside fear and ventured out between the two walls of water after Moses parted the Red Sea? Think about Noah, who built an ark, not even knowing what it was but trusting that his family would indeed be saved if he followed God's instructions. Abraham, when asked to sacrifice his only son, did not withhold his precious child from the Lord. Instead, he was willing to give him over to God, not knowing that, thankfully, the hand of the Lord would stop him.

There are so many other stories I could reference, but I will summarize with what the Bible says in Hebrews chapter 11, oftentimes referred to as the Hall of Faith:

And what more shall I say? I do not have time to tell about Gideon, Barak, Samson and Jephthah, about David and Samuel and the prophets, who through faith conquered kingdoms, administered justice, and gained what was promised; who shut the mouths of lions, quenched the fury of the flames, and escaped the edge of the sword; whose weakness was turned to strength; and who became powerful in battle and routed foreign armies. Women received back their dead, raised to life again. There were others who were tortured, refusing to be released so that they might gain an even better resurrection. Some faced jeers and flogging, and even chains and imprisonment. They were put to death by stoning; they were sawed in two; they were killed by the sword. They went about in sheepskins and goatskins, destitute, persecuted and mistreated—the world was not worthy of them. They wandered in deserts and mountains, living in caves and in holes in the ground. (Hebrews 11:32-38)

This is the kind of life God calls us to live. I've said it before, and I'll say it again. Our God is a crazy God. If we're following Him, crazy should be the norm in our lives. If our lives don't look like the radical, sold-out lives of God's followers in the Bible, then maybe we aren't following the same God.

The thing about big, bold, radical steps of faith for God is that they lead us to big, bold, radical places with God. God is not a safe and predictable deity. In fact, He likes to do wild, crazy things that grab people's attention and demand an audience. To some degree, the power of God we see at work in our lives is limited by the amount of faith we have. We open ourselves up to seeing God's majesty when we trust Him with the big things in our life.

The more space we give Him, the more room He has to work.

Following Jesus is awesome. Terrifying, sometimes, but always awesome. One thing I'm learning is the promises God makes often only come as a result of choosing to leave the safety of the shore and dive into the waves of the storm. Just as the Israelites had to cross the Red Sea in order to reach the Promised Land, often we have our own brave steps we need to take before God can fulfill in us what He wants to accomplish.

American aerospace engineer Burt Rutan said, "The day before something is a breakthrough, it's a crazy idea." Burt's words summarized my exact thoughts on the day I realized God was calling me to quit my job in order to pursue writing and speaking fulltime: "This is a crazy idea!" Here's an excerpt from my journal the morning I resigned:

Monday morning, August 18, 2014

Words seem to escape me. My heart races and palms sweat at the mere thought of what I am about to do. I try to prepare my thoughts, but my mind has turned to mush. "What am I doing?" I question myself. "Am I making the biggest mistake of my life? What if I'm wrong?"

These fears and more swirl about in my brain as I try to muster up one ounce of courage to plunge forward into the unknown.

Over the past several months, I have heard God speak to me time and time again, yet once more, doubt rolls over like an ocean wave threatening to drown me in the seas of uncertainty. I concentrate on His voice echoing in my mind, "To the faithful, I am faithful."

I want to be faithful. I just never guessed being faithful would look like this. I have played out this day in my mind before, but never once did the scenario require so much courage. I never dreamed there would be so much at stake. I never imagined it would require so much... faith.

Now the only thing I cling to is my hope in Him. There is nothing left. Nothing remains but Him. Why shouldn't I follow and give Him everything? Why shouldn't I go "all in?" The truth is I am too far gone. There is no turning back. He stole my heart and gave me the tiniest glimpse of His love. I can't say "no" now. There is no other choice. Besides, it is my own fault I am here. After all, I did say, "Anything. I will do anything." These words tumble around in my mind as fresh as the day I spoke them four years ago. But now they mingle with new words, new promises I've made, and new requests I've placed before Him. "God," I said, "I want people to look at my life and say, 'That's just crazy. How great is her God?'"

Well, I've learned my lesson. It seems God likes to answer bold, radical prayers, and He loves making His followers look crazy for His namesake. Crazy... ha, well this sure feels crazy. It's definitely the craziest thing I've ever done. Like twelve crazy men some two thousand years ago, I am making the same crazy decision to leave everything and follow one crazy, big God.

Today, I am resigning from my job. I feel much like the fisherman Simon pulling my boat up on the shore only to leave it all there at the edge of the water. I don't know where I'm going. I don't know what the future holds or how to get there. But I do know one thing: Jesus is leading. He held out His hand and said, "Come." What could I possibly do but follow? I am excited about this new journey and terrified at the same time. In all my years, I have never felt more certain about a decision yet so unsure of the outcome. Hmm... I guess that's why they call it faith.[+]

Proverbs 19:21 says, "Many are the plans in a person's heart, but it is the Lord's purpose that prevails." David and I were planning to wait until it made sense financially for me to quit my job, but God said, "I want you to do the craziest thing possible." For me, that was leaving my job in the middle of the year, forgoing my annual bonus,

+ You can read more from my journal on page 31 of the complimentary guide *Plan Your ESCAPE*. You can download it for FREE at HeatherRaeHutzel.com/PlanYourEscape

while not knowing how we would be sustained without half of our family income. We couldn't live on David's salary forever. God would have to stand in the gap. And stand in the gap He has!

God continues to amaze us month by month as bills are paid and needs are met, but more importantly, God has shown us both something so powerful. When you are living in God's Story and following in His footsteps, He confirms it for you all along the way. Like the time I witnessed what I consider to be a miracle.

The month I started working from home, our water bill went up. A lot. It more than quadrupled! We were surprised the bill would change so drastically but just assumed it was the cost of me working from home. We still believed God would take care of us since He was the one who called me to quit my job.

Four months later, the water bill continued to increase. It wasn't until David finally did the math that we realized something wasn't adding up. We had a leak.

After multiple visits from the county and a plumber, we were given the verdict. The county is only responsible for three feet off the water main by the street; everything else is considered our responsibility. What was likely only a small hole somewhere along the water line was going to run us anywhere from a couple thousand to *several* thousand dollars!

As the county workers spent hours digging up the front yard, I quickly realized, they were unearthing a lot more than three feet of dirt. If they hadn't found the leak yet, it was definitely on our property. That's when I started praying.

"God, I believe You are the one who called me to quit my job, and I believe that You will provide for us. It's not looking good. I honestly don't know how You can fix this. It seems impossible. But you are the God of the impossible. I know that even if we have to pay to fix the leak, You will still continue to provide. I trust You."

Not long after that conversation with God, the county worker came to the front door.

"We found the leak," he said. "It's eight feet off the water main…"

My heart sank.

"But," he continued, "We just went ahead and fixed it for you since we are here and have the ground open. Everything should be good now."

I wish I could share all the miraculous, wonderful, and powerful ways God has shown up in our lives since I quit my job, but I can't keep track of them all! I try to write them down, but there are far too many. As a matter of fact, I've adopted a new phrase on this journey, "God is so ridiculously good." He truly is so faithful. No matter what He calls you to, no matter how crazy or illogical it may seem, trust Him. It is only when we choose to live a life that *requires* miracles that we will actually see them.

Now that doesn't mean it's been smooth sailing since we've stepped out into the sea. We've had stormy moments since I quit my job, and I know there are still more to come, but as it says in James chapter 1:

I consider it pure joy whenever I face trials of many kinds, because I know that the testing of my faith produces perseverance. And I must let perseverance finish its work so that I can be mature and complete, not lacking anything. (James 1:2-4)

I'll be honest. Trials and storms suck. They really do. Sometimes the only thing that carries me through is the thought that I will somehow be stronger and more like Jesus on the other side. Some of the hardest prayers I pray are when I say, "God, I don't want to work on my character flaws. I don't want to go through this difficult learning experience. I don't want to face this problem, but I really, *really* want to be like You. Do whatever You have to do. Change my perception of the storm as only You can." (God loves our dangerous prayers!)

Then next time, when the storms arise, I remember that I asked to be more like Jesus, and Jesus was never the kind of guy to sail around a storm. He always went straight through them.

I am a firm believer that God doesn't cause storms. God is good. He only creates good things, and, thankfully, He is more than capable of creating something good out of bad, stormy circumstances.

We have to remember, while God has a plan and purpose for or lives, there is also an enemy who has a plan and purpose for our lives—to keep us separated from God.

Imagine the negative consequences on a person's life if they believed God caused their storms. That's a sure way to separate someone from God. Instead of causing storms, our God is always ready to take the enemy's tactics and throw them right back in his face. Our Captain is able to lead us through the enemy's storms and make us stronger and more Christ-like on the other side.

As Joseph said from his royal position, received only after facing a lifetime of troubles, "You intended to harm me, but God intended it for good to accomplish what is now being done" (Genesis 50:20).

God knows the shortest distance between two points is a straight line. We can sail around our storms, but the quickest and surest way to reach the Promised Land is to set our heading straight ahead, directly into the wind and waves.

**

Friend, I can promise you, one day Jesus is going to ask you to do something radical. (And if you follow Jesus for any length of time, it will likely happen more than once!) It won't make sense. It will seem crazy, but that's why it's called faith.

I wish I could say this journey of following Jesus gets easier, but unfortunately, it is usually the case that the opposite is true. If we are doing this "Jesus-thing" right, it will only get more difficult. Here's the good news: while our difficulties and challenges don't go away, neither does our God.

God doesn't call us to places where He hasn't already walked. He is a crazy God writing a radical story about an out-of-this-world kingdom (literally). The Kingdom of God is at hand (Mark 1:15). If you are ready to embrace God's Story, you have to be ready to embrace a whole lot of radical!

God is still looking for regular, ordinary people who are ready and willing to do crazy, extraordinary things. God is not finished writing His Story, and He is certainly not finished writing yours. Each and every day, God gives us an opportunity to partner with Him, to choose something that feels just a little bit crazy in order that we might tell an amazing story with our lives.[+]

+ For discussion questions for this chapter, check out page 34 in the complimentary guide *Plan Your ESCAPE*. You can download it for FREE at HeatherRaeHutzel.com/PlanYourEscape

CHAPTER 11

CHARACTER

[kar-ik-ter]
noun

1. the aggregate of features and traits that form the
individual nature of some person or thing:
*"It was a lifetime of relationships and experiences
that molded his character."*

I absolutely despised writing when I was younger,
so imagine my surprise when at age twenty-four
I sensed a calling to write a book. (Talk about
crazy.)[+] Imagine the even bigger surprise of
publishing that novel a year and a half later and

+ Read about uncovering your purpose on page 35 of the complimentary guide
Plan Your ESCAPE. You can download it for FREE at
HeatherRaeHutzel.com/PlanYourEscape

feeling the desire to write more books. My life had radically shifted.

As someone with no formal training, I learned a great deal about writing first-hand while penning my debut novel. For example, in fiction writing, authors tend to classify themselves into two main categories: "plotters" and "pantsers." A plotter is someone who takes the time to create an outline and craft a plot before sitting down to write the main prose of the story. A pantser is someone who, as you might have guessed, flies by the seat of their pants. Knowing the backstory of my first book, it is probably no surprise that I identify with the latter group.

My "seat-of-the-pants" writing style became even more obvious to me as I began working on my second novel. When sitting down to write, I would have at least a vague idea of how the characters should behave in a particular scene. I could imagine how they would feel, perform, and interact, but something very strange would always happen. Without warning, my characters would take on a completely different persona than I intended. At times, they acted irrationally and went places where I never planned to send them. Before my very eyes the characters came to life and took control of the story. They became real people.

Now, while I don't plot my fiction books, there are particular events I have in mind from the beginning that I know are supposed to take place. I do have an ultimate end goal for the characters. The challenge of writing in this style is the constant redirection of the characters back to the main parts of the story. In a sense, I give the characters free will to become real people and take on the various roles they desire, but all along I must continually course-correct to ensure the characters reach their ultimate fulfillment in the final scene.

This is the way God works with us. As the author of His Story, God is responsible for the development of our character, but contrary to what many Christians believe, God is not a plotter. God does not preordain our lives, but rather gives us free will to become real people, not robots. God's desire is to watch us become the character He's always known we could be. Like any good pantser, God is constantly course-correcting, guiding us through the story, pointing us to the main events, and ultimately leading us to the final chapter. God may be the author of this story, but He wants *you* to help write it.

This is the journey we are on and the story in which we live. We are all characters in a story that is far more grand than our own. While the plot has many twists and turns, there is an end goal after which we seek. There is a character that is meant to be developed within us and a final chapter at which we must arrive. Our destination and great treasure is this: knowing God's character and seeking to be like Him.

Now, while we've already identified God's character as simply "love," God has many layers, layers we should be eager to peel back as we seek to discover more and more about His character. There is only one way we can be like Him and that is to know Him.

God created us with an innate desire to explore Him. Whether we recognize it or not, humans always want to know more, not only about God and His Word, but also His world. Truth be told, all matters of science, mathematics, and art are the result of a deep study of the character of God. Whether realized or not, every scientist who has ever devoted time and energy to his field of interest has systematically and intensely studied the character of God's existence. The same is true for mathematics, art, and other subjects concerning the physical realm. Somehow, these topics we tend to look at separately are intricately woven together to form a magnificent tapestry which is a reflection of God.

The summation of all we know collectively as the human race is a mere fraction of the grandeur of God's wisdom which we were created to discover. Yet sadly, many spend their entire lives searching, exploring, and pursuing their passions, yet never once realizing or understanding it was the very character of God after which they sought.

We were made to seek after and desire all things God. We were created to seek His wisdom because it is in His infinite wisdom that we see His love. All the intricacies of God have been put into place for one sole purpose—us.

We are the object of God's creation, and therefore, the object of His love. All things in creation, known and unknown, create a line—a line that points to God, the magnificent designer—but the other end of the line is perhaps the most revealing factor. The other end of the line points to us.

While God's creation was made by Him, through Him, and for Him, it was made with us in mind. Who can discover the great vastness of the physical realm? No one can, although we may spend our whole lives trying. Eternity in Christ grants us this deepest longing to know Him and know all He is. He is all things combined, seen and unseen.

The fact that there is a realm unseen to the human eye is unimaginable. The grand intricacy of how an unknown world may interact with the one we live in is far too much to grasp. It is simply too much for the human mind to wrap around. The grandeur of God can never be conceived, but He will reveal Himself when we seek Him.

The part of God's character He reveals to us is His infinitely vast wisdom and reality. The more we know Him, the more we realize just how little we know about Him. How could anything be more amazing or enticing than the incomprehensible existence of God? It's like trying to wrap a simple human mind around the concept of infinity. We cannot even begin to imagine coming to fully know the One who has no end to His love or existence, yet we have all of eternity to try.

For this is what we were created to do—explore the grandeur of God—all along falling more and more in love with Him as we realize that each and every uncovered truth points to Him and simultaneously back at us.

It is when we discover the character of God that we discover who we were made to be. Our journey of uncovering the character of Yahweh is simultaneously a journey of uncovering our own identity. It is in those moments when we begin to excavate the truth that our character is developed, and we are formed into image bearers like our hero, Jesus.

To be like God is to make a decision to be like Jesus. To be like Jesus is to choose to continuously escape from the Story of the World and embrace a radical, set-apart life. It's a life of escaping and embracing, repenting and believing.

As we venture further with Jesus on this journey, we begin to realize that our bodies are burdened and heavily laden with various types of chains that encumber us from our time of slavery. Addictions, fears, sinful patterns, and grudges are merely a small representation of the shackles we have allowed to bind us during our time of enslavement. While we may be living outside our prison cells, following Jesus farther and farther away from the prison compound that once held us hostage, without even realizing, we carry these old chains with us. Rather than shedding and dropping them into a heap on the floor of our cell, we leave them bound securely around our ankles, wrists, and neck. Jesus may have set us free, we may have escaped the cell, but in so many areas of our lives, we still choose to live as a slave.

These chains create a problem. They limit us in our ability to follow and look like Jesus. They hinder our character development. Rather than being able to run after Jesus at full speed, we are condemned to shuffle behind Him or crawl on our hands and knees, dragging these shackles that weigh us down. We can't move as fast as Jesus does. We have to stop more often. We get bloodied and battered each time a chain catches on an obstacle standing in the way. There are days we can't move at all because the burdens we carry are far too much to endure. It's hard for us to follow Jesus out upon the waters when we are bearing the weight of an anchor around our neck. We will sink straight to the bottom and drown.

As we embrace our part in God's Story, we will not only peel back the layers of God to discover more of His character, we will also peel back our own layers. We will strip away our chains to reveal the trueness of who we are: our identity and character in God's Story.

Each of us, who bears the image of God and His Spirit within us, is like a stone made for the temple of God. We are part of a greater whole, but each stone has a specific role or purpose to fulfill. Each of us has a unique character role to play in God's Story. There is a place within the temple, the Church body, where God wants to place you, but first, He has to shape you to fit that space.

Our chains are the pieces of us that don't look like Jesus. They are the pieces God wants to break away so we can reflect Him more perfectly and fulfill our role more fully. We must allow the hand of God to chip and chisel away at us because He alone can form us and reveal the image hiding underneath.

As I think of God shaping us as stones to be used in the building of some great structure, I am reminded of the famous Renaissance artist Michelangelo. Once, when asked how he created his masterpiece the statue of David, he reportedly said, "It was easy. I just chipped away the stone that didn't look like David."

This is what God is doing with each and every one of us. He is chipping away at every piece of us that doesn't look like Jesus. With each strike of his hammer against the metal chisel, He is working to set free a masterpiece that is buried inside.

The best part is that the sculpture God is working to reveal doesn't look like you or me. It doesn't even look like a glorified version of ourselves with the hard lines of carved muscle seen on the statue of David. No, like any work of art, the end result looks remarkably different than the raw materials with which the artist started. In this case, the final result the artist is striving to achieve is an image that looks exactly like Him.

Now, of course we won't all be "Christian clones" without any personality of our own. In fact, the opposite is true. We will still be uniquely "us." I once heard it said that discipleship is the process of becoming the person Jesus would be if He were you.

However, in our sin-filled and fallen world, we do not and cannot perfectly reflect God's image. This is the difference between us and Jesus. Jesus was pure, spotless, blameless, and without sin. He had to be because only a human without sin could perfectly reflect an all Holy God.

It's hard for us to wrap our minds around the idea that Jesus came to re-ascribe our identity as God's image bearers, because while the trueness of our identity and character is complete in the spiritual realm, it is not yet fully manifested in our physical realm.

We are sinners, but because of what Jesus did, our sins have been wiped away. When God looks at us, He sees us like Jesus, even though the world still looks at us and sees our mistakes and shortcomings. That's why the Bible says in 2 Corinthians 3:18 that we are "being transformed into His image with ever-increasing glory." While our Spirit on the inside looks just like God (because it *is* the Spirit of God), our physical self, character, and image are still being continually transformed to look more and more like Him.

With each layer we cast off, we unleash a deeper understanding of both God and ourselves. Because we have been made in His image, each layer we remove is symbolic of throwing off another shackle of our enslavement and, simultaneously, uncovering another level of God's love for us. With God's help, we are unveiling the perfection of His image that is tucked away within us, a perfection that is only completed when we unite together.

***

In the Gospels, Jesus tells His followers to *seek* the Kingdom of God. Many people, however, misquote this phrase as, "*build* the Kingdom of

God." This distinction might not seem significant, but it is.

We don't need to build the Kingdom of God, because it already exists. Jesus said, "The Kingdom of God is at hand. Repent and believe the good news" (Mark 1:15)! The Kingdom of God is already here, but like our precious temple, the body of Christ, the Kingdom is buried among the deception and fictional Story of the World. This is why, when talking about the Church, I say, *"rebuild* the temple" not "build it." We aren't working from scratch. The pieces and stones for the temple are already here, but we need to search for them among the rubble and bring them back together. We need to unearth the stones, chip away at the sharp, jagged pieces and roughly hewn edges, and reveal the hidden image of the cornerstone, the strong foundation, Jesus.

Think about it, even a cardboard structure assembled by a child would be sturdier when rooted on a solid foundation, but what happens when the storms and winds come? If the framing, walls, and roof of the structure are built of a subpar material to the foundation, the structure will never stand.

As the temple of our God, we need to be united and strong, a place where everyone feels welcome to come in and find escape from the storms of this fallen world. Our character needs to look like Jesus. We need to be Jesus to the world.

It's time for the Church to start behaving as if the Holy God of the universe is actually living inside of us because, guess what, HE IS. We need to stop living as if God is "up there" and, instead, bring Him "down here." This has always been the role of the Church: to continue the manifestation of the life of Christ here on earth.

Callings are not created; they are given. God has a calling for your life, a character part He wants you to fulfill. While that very specific responsibility might manifest itself differently at various stages in your life, there is one clear role God has for everyone: to reflect His character.

This is the purpose of our time here on earth: to fully escape from our imprisonment as anything other than the image bearers we were created to be. To help others recognize their own need for escape, unite together as the temple of God, and chip away at each other so we can fully embrace our freedom, not only in the life to come, but also in the here and now.[+]

> In every block of marble I see a statue as plain as though it stood before me, shaped and perfect in attitude and action. I have only to hew away the rough walls that imprison the lovely apparition to reveal it to the other eyes as mine see it.—Michelangelo

---

[+] For discussion questions for this chapter, check out page 37 in the complimentary guide *Plan Your ESCAPE*. You can download it for FREE at HeatherRaeHutzel.com/PlanYourEscape

CHAPTER 12

COST

[kawst, kost]
noun

1. the price paid to acquire, produce, accomplish, or maintain anything; a sacrifice, loss, or penalty:
"He knew this journey would cost him something; he just wasn't sure what it would be."

ollowing Jesus (like really following Him) is not for the faint of heart. There is only one reason to follow Jesus: to be like Him. As we continue on this journey of faith, we have to ask ourselves a very important question. "Do we want to be like Jesus in every way?"

This is the goal after all.

Jesus didn't live an easy life. In fact, it was downright difficult. We need to be prepared to not just answer the question, "Do we want to be like Jesus?" but also, "Do we still want to be like Him when it gets hard, even when it costs us something?"

We need to realize that this thing called "following Jesus" is not going to be laid-back and stress-free. Nowhere in the Bible does it say this journey will be without trials. Instead, Jesus tells us the very opposite: "In this world, you will have trouble," (John 16:33). Yet amazingly (somehow, someway), so many of us have still managed to water-down His words.

Mark Batterson says it this way in his book *All In*:

I'm afraid we've cheapened the gospel by allowing people to buy in without selling out. We've made it too convenient, too comfortable. We've given people just enough Jesus to be bored but not enough to feel the surge of holy adrenaline that courses through your veins when you decide to follow Him no matter what, no matter where, no matter when.

He goes on to say:

You cannot be in the presence of God and be bored at the same time. For that matter, you cannot be in the will of God and be bored at the same time. If you follow in the footsteps of Jesus, it will be anything but boring.[1]

It's true. The journey of living in God's Story is amazing. It's the adventure of a lifetime! We must remember though, if we've said "anything" to God, it means "anything." That "anything" will start small, but trust me, it will continue to expand until, one day, "anything" is equal to "all of you." This journey will cost you something, and that something will be your life.

We've been fooled, sweet Church. God doesn't just want our hearts; He wants our whole selves. Every single piece. Our entire lives. He's already given us His whole self, and I can promise you this—He'd do it all over again.

***

Ever since that moment when I gave God the "all in" card, He has been upping the ante and calling my husband, David, and me to bigger and more challenging "anythings." It was one of our more recent "anythings," though, that has proven to be one of the most difficult.

In the fall of 2015, Crossroads, the church we attend, kicked off a three-year campaign called "I'm In" to fund the various initiatives we run after–things like eliminating poverty in our city, liberating girls from sex slavery in India, abolishing the AIDS epidemic in South Africa, and ensuring that people

1. Batterson, Mark. *All In: You Are One Decision Away from a Totally Different Life*. Grand Rapids, MI: Zondervan, 2013.

all over the globe have access to the gospel in a way that makes sense.

These initiatives excite me and fill me with hope for our world. So as David and I began to talk about our financial commitment, I offered up a similar prayer to the one I first prayed five years ago.

"God," I said, "I'm in. I'll do anything. You still have all of me."

God replied, "Really? Well that's good to know. I'm so glad you are still willing to do anything." I sensed Him smiling. (Actually, now that I think about it, it was probably more like a smirk.)

"Yes, really. I'm in," I responded. "So what do You want us to give to this campaign? You know more than anyone that money is really tight. But we trust You, God. How much money do You want us to commit?"

God paused. "Heather, do you really love Me?"

"Of course, God!"

"Do you really trust Me?"

"Yes, I really do!"

Another pause. "Heather, what if I asked you for all of it?"

Now it was my turn to be silent. "Uh… what do You mean *all of it*?"

"What if I ask for every penny you have? What if I literally want you to go 'all in?' Would you still do anything?"

I wish I could tell you my immediate response was, "Yes, here! Take it all!" It wasn't that easy, though. I didn't feel like God was specifically asking for our entire savings, but He was definitely questioning whether or not it was "on the table." Would we really go all in?

I wrestled with God. Financial generosity has never been a source of struggle for me, but something was different now.

At the time this campaign began, I had been self-employed for a little over a year, but income was still a struggle. David once jokingly called my business venture a "non-profit." It's not, but that gives you a sense of the situation. God called me to quit my job, yet here I was, a year later, still not making any money. Add this to a husband's salary that doesn't cover all of our monthly bills, and things get a bit dicey.

Fortunately, thanks to some smart saving in the first four years of our marriage, we had a nice little cushion tucked away in our bank account. It had become our safety net and the buffer to make up the difference every month in income.

Now, God was asking for it.

I didn't want to give it. I didn't want to commit our entire savings account to our church campaign. Having that money made me feel safe and protected, and it ensured that I could work at least another few months without pay. While my head told me, "Our God is faithful and He will provide," my heart wasn't one-hundred percent certain He would. So in the midst of this journey I had a really raw conversation with God about what it means to be obedient to Him even when it costs us something big. It went a little something like this:

Me: "I feel like a phony, God."

God: "What do you mean?"

Me: "Sometimes, You ask me to do things I really don't want to do. Like this thing with the campaign."

God: "Go on."

Me: "But when you ask me to do these types of things, I end up doing them anyway."

God: "So, what's the problem?"

Me: "Well, because I don't *want* to do some of the things you ask me to do. Sometimes, I'm even miserable in the midst of actually doing it."

God: "I see."

Me: "Yeah, and sometimes, people compliment me for doing these things, or even worse, tell me I impacted their life in some way."

God: "How awful," He said with a smirk.

Me: "Yeah, it is. Because I feel like a phony."

God: "Let me ask you a question."

Me: "Okay."

God: "Do you think I wanted to be murdered? Do you think I liked the idea of dying a horrendously painful and gruesome death?"

Me: I lowered my head, "No."

God: "Obedience is simply following the desires and wishes of another." He tipped my chin upward and looked into my eyes. "It has nothing to do with whether or not you 'feel' like doing it. In fact, the greater the discomfort, the bigger the sacrifice. As you know, I'm all about giving for the sake of others. Sometimes, the feelings come later, after you've made the sacrifice. Other times, they don't. There will be times when you discover you actually enjoy the things I have called you to do. Other times, it will cost you something great. Occasionally, you will understand why I have asked you to do certain things, but more often, you won't find out until you finish this life. All I want is for you to say 'yes' to me. 'Not my will, Father, but Yours.' Regardless, of whether or not you want to do it, just do it. That's not phony. That's obedience."

David and I prayed about our financial commitment. We sought God on the number He actually wanted us to give. Did God really want our entire savings? Or was He merely testing our obedience like Abraham?

It was only after we came to the place of saying, "Yes, God. Even if the 'anything' You want is all the money we have," that we thought we knew the number God wanted us to give.

He wanted it all.

We made a commitment that in three years' time we would give a dollar amount equal to the funds we had in our bank account when the campaign first began. We offered everything we had, and with it we said, "God, there is no possible way to meet this commitment unless You come through. We can't do this unless You supernaturally provide for us. We want to fulfill this commitment. We need Your help. We trust You. You have all of us. *We will do anything.*"

This has been one of the hardest things God has asked of me to date, yet I have a supernatural peace. It is quite literally a peace that surpasses my understanding.

What I once knew only in my head, I now believe fully in my heart. God works in an upside down, counter-cultural kind of way. While the world may think trials and struggles are nothing but a source of unrest and turmoil, our God has a way of flipping these trials upside down and turning them into the very places where we find peace.

Peace is not the absence of a storm; it's the calm you find when you realize Jesus is standing beside you in the midst of the storm.

Romans 5:3-4 says we "glory in our sufferings, because we know that suffering produces perseverance; perseverance, character; and character, hope."

If we follow a Jesus-looking God, it will require a sacrifice. Following Jesus will undoubtedly cost us something at some point. The question we have to ask ourselves is, "How far will we go to be like Him?"

Are we willing to sacrifice all for the All in All? Do we want to be like Him in every way? Like when Jesus hung out with the social outcasts? Or how about when He challenged the religious people of the day? What about when He traveled to spread the gospel with no knowledge of where He would find His next meal or lay His head at night? How about when He was labeled a lunatic, a heretic, and a drunkard? What about when He was mocked? Spit on? Beaten? Would you follow Him that far? Would you follow Him to the cross? If we want to be like Jesus, then we must be willing to say, "I am ready to die."

Jesus said it this way,

> Whoever wants to be my disciple must deny themselves and take up their cross and follow me. For whoever wants to save their life will lose it, but whoever loses their life for me will find it. What good will it be for someone to gain the whole world, yet forfeit their soul? (Matthew 16:24-26)

I think sometimes we gloss over the words of the Gospels, thinking, "Surely Jesus didn't mean what He said." Oh, but surely He did. In the first century Church, there were plenty of people who were willing to take up their cross, or worse, take up the stake where they would be burned, or the pole upon which they would be impaled, or the den of lions into which they would be thrown.

"Our normal is so subnormal that normal seems radical," says Mark Batterson in his book *All In*. "To the first-century disciples, normal and radical were synonyms." He goes on to say, "It's time to quit living as if the purpose of life is to arrive safely at death… Jesus didn't die to keep us safe. He died to make us dangerous."

The disciples understood that when Jesus said there is a cost involved in following Him, He meant it. For example, the Apostle Paul totally understood what it meant to sail through the storm, literally and figuratively! He said:

I have worked much harder, been in prison more frequently, been flogged more severely, and been exposed to death again and again. Five times I received from the Jews the forty lashes minus one. Three times I was beaten with rods, once I was pelted with stones, three times I was shipwrecked, I spent a night and a day in the open sea, I have been constantly on the move. I have been in danger from rivers, in danger from bandits, in danger from my fellow Jews, in danger from Gentiles; in danger in the city, in danger in the country, in danger at sea; and in danger from false believers. I have labored and toiled and have often gone without sleep; I have known hunger and thirst and have often gone without food; I have been cold and naked. Besides everything else, I face daily the pressure of my concern for all the churches. (2 Corinthians 11:23-28)

Dang. "Poor Paul," we might say. No, Paul knew what he was getting himself into. Paul understood the cost of following a crazy, radical God. Do we? Following a crazy, radical God requires crazy, radical sacrifice that comes when we step out into unchartered waters and stormy seas. We do this all for the sake of what lies on the other side—the Promised Land—a life that more completely and perfectly reflects the character of the Almighty God, a life that is radical and oh so very set-apart.[+]

+ For discussion questions for this chapter, check out page 38 in the complimentary guide *Plan Your ESCAPE*. You can download it for FREE at HeatherRaeHutzel.com/PlanYourEscape

CHAPTER 13

CALL

[kawl]
verb

1. to ask or invite to come:
"The hero's call to adventure was not what he expected."

I t happened to a young peasant girl named Mary. It took place in the life of a Christian-killer called Paul. It occurred one day to a brazen fisherman named Simon, and at some point in your life, it will happen to you.

One day, Jesus is going to call *you* to do something.

This goes far beyond removing our chains or acts of obedience. This isn't God simply asking you to make a change in your life. This isn't just a call to reflect Him more. This is THE CALL. This is the moment when God calls you, not just to follow Him, but to carry on ahead of Him. This is the moment when God bestows upon you a mission— His mission. It will undoubtedly shape you and mold you, and yes, it will definitely require radical obedience and the stripping off of your chains. It is not separate from your journey; it is the culmination of your journey.

While God's desire and purpose for each of us as a part of His Story is similar, that is, He calls us all to be with Him and be like Him, God does have a unique role He desires each of us to play. There is a place amidst the temple wall that only you can fill. Experiencing the call of God and discovering that role is the journey.[+]

I once had a friend say to me that he was okay with being mediocre. That statement struck me.

I'm okay with being mediocre.

This friend was basically saying he was fine with putting forth average effort in order to live an average life. It made me think, "Am I okay with being mediocre?"

The answer was a resounding "no." I'm not at all okay with being mediocre, and I hope you aren't either. We know from studying God's Story that we are made for more. As the body of Christ, the Church, we have an enormous role to play in God's Story. We have a purpose and a mission, and it is the farthest thing from being mediocre or average.

+ Read about a way to discover your passion on page 39 of the complimentary guide *Plan Your ESCAPE*. You can download it for FREE at HeatherRaeHutzel.com/PlanYourEscape

We are called to be set-apart and different. We are a holy people and a royal priesthood, and there is nothing average or ordinary about that.

God wants us to live the life He always intended for us to have—a life buried deep within the story of God. It is a story that reflects the image of our Heavenly Father and King. It is an existence that bears the mission of Jesus. It is a life that says "anything" to a God who said "anything" to us. It is the life of a disciple, a follower of Christ.

In the same way Jesus once called twelve average men to come and follow Him, Jesus calls regular ol' us to be a part of the same amazing journey. When we look at ourselves, we see nothing special. Heck, when the world looks at us, it sees nothing special. But when God looks at us, He sees past the plain, dull hunk of rock we are on the outside and envisions the formed masterpiece of an image that looks like Him on the inside.

Jesus had this same insight when choosing His first twelve representatives. He saw something unique and special in all of them, but one in particular stood out from the rest. Check out the story of Simon.

> One day as Jesus was standing by the Lake of Gennesaret, the people were crowding around him and listening to the word of God. He saw at the water's edge two boats, left there by the fishermen, who were washing their nets. He got into one of the boats, the one belonging to Simon, and asked him to put out a little from shore.

Then he sat down and taught the people from the boat.

When he had finished speaking, he said to Simon, "Put out into deep water, and let down the nets for a catch."

Simon answered, "Master, we've worked hard all night and haven't caught anything. But because you say so, I will let down the nets."

When they had done so, they caught such a large number of fish that their nets began to break. So they signaled their partners in the other boat to come and help them, and they came and filled both boats so full that they began to sink.

When Simon Peter saw this, he fell at Jesus' knees and said, "Go away from me, Lord; I am a sinful man!" For he and all his companions were astonished at the catch of fish they had taken, and so were James and John, the sons of Zebedee, Simon's partners.

Then Jesus said to Simon, "Don't be afraid; from now on you will fish for people." So they pulled their boats up on shore, left everything and followed him. (Luke 5:1-11)

Jesus saw potential in Simon. He saw commitment, determination, hope, zeal, obedience, and faith. When Jesus was teaching on the shore, only two boats remained. Simon and his partners had fished all night, despite catching nothing. They were the last to bring their boats back into shore.

They didn't give up easily. Fishermen didn't wash their nets unless they planned to go back out the next day. They had an unwavering commitment and determination that was fueled by the hope of success when they went out again tomorrow. Jesus saw these qualities in the way Simon worked, but there were other characteristics Jesus desired to be present in His disciples. Simon had these qualities, but they were hidden. Jesus decided to draw them out.

The first test we must pass when we are called by God is the test of willingness. Are we ready to do what God calls us to do? Simon was. Simon allowed Jesus to use his resources for God's work. He willingly offered up his boat when Jesus asked to borrow it in order to teach. Little did Simon know he was about to become the visual aid for Jesus' sermon.

After teaching the crowds from his place in the boat, Jesus asked Simon to do something that sounded a little crazy: "Put out into deep water, and let down the nets for a catch" (Luke 5:4).

Simon was tired. He had been working overtime and had nothing to show for it. Not only that, but Simon and his partners had been working during primetime hours. Fish were active during the night, not during the heat of the day. Simon was a fisherman. He knew the trade, yet here was a carpenter–turned-rabbi who was trying to tell him how to do his job. It didn't make sense.

When Jesus calls you to help Him write the story of your life, I can promise you, there will be things He asks of you that don't make sense. There will be times when God challenges you in an area where you are very knowledgeable. He will ask you to do it a "bass-ackwards" way that you just know, deep down in the core of your being, will never work. *He's going to ask you to do it anyway.*

He's going to challenge you to take a risk, to put out into "deep water." He'll tell you to let down your nets, give it everything you have. He'll ask you to pour all of your resources into this test: your time, your money, your heart... He will request you give everything you have to a calling that doesn't make a lick of sense. Oh yeah, and chances are good, like Simon, there will be a crowd of people watching. You might look like a fool. You might lose your money, your reputation, your family, friends, job... you might even lose your life.

We have to ask ourselves, can we, like Mary, who was essentially asked to soil her reputation in order to bring forth the Son of God, say, "I am the Lord's servant. May your word to me be fulfilled" (Luke 1:38).

Mary was a decent, upright girl in her day, yet she was willing to cast aside the appearance of worldly "holiness" in order to experience a truly set-apart life. Because of her decision, her devotion to God was questioned by everyone except the One who really mattered. Sometimes, in revealing our truest, deepest commitment to our King, it appears the opposite to the outside world. We must continually ask ourselves, "In what story are we living? Are we trying to win the approval of God or our fellow man" (Galatians 1:10)?

When God comes to us, asking us to do the most absurd thing we can imagine (with an audience watching), how will we respond? If we are truly living in God's Story, then we, like Simon, will say, "God, this is crazy! It doesn't make any sense, *but because You say so*, I will do it."

I believe these are the sweet words God longs to hear from all of His people. "But because you say so." These are the words that put "anything" into action. "Anything" means nothing until it is transformed from the words on our lips to the actions of our hands.[+]

Psalm 18:25 says God is faithful to those who are faithful to Him. This means that while we are taking big, bold, radical steps of faith toward God, He steps in and pours out big, bold, radical blessings.

I once heard John Gray, Associate Pastor at Lakewood Church, say, "God wants to put His 'super' on top of your 'natural.'" As a Christ-follower, we must remember we are not just human; we are also Spirit. It is the Holy Spirit inside of us that adds the "super" to our "natural" and gives us strength to trust and obey our radical God. Not only that, it is this same God who also takes our normal, natural human abilities and turns them into something super-natural and amazingly extraordinary.

God places His Holy Spirit inside us for two reasons: to be with us and to work through us. The Bible tells us the Holy Spirit of God is a deposit that

---

+ Read more from my journal on page 41 of the complimentary guide *Plan Your ESCAPE*. You can download it for FREE at HeatherRaeHutzel.com/PlanYourEscape

has been placed in our care (2 Corinthians 1:22). It is a deposit for which God will one day return. The Spirit of God that resides in us is an investment, and like the parable of the talents, God wants to receive a return.

In Matthew 25, Jesus tells a parable about a man who entrusts some of his financial resources to his servants while away on a journey. Some versions of this story say he gave the servants bags of gold, others say he gave them "talents," a denomination of money, like a coin. The man called on three of his servants. One servant was entrusted with five talents, another received two, and the third servant received one. The story says the man gave to his servants according to their ability.

The parable tells how the first two servants immediately put the money to work in order to gain a return on their master's investment. The story doesn't say what they did. Perhaps they invested the money, or maybe they purchased raw materials to create goods they could sell. We don't know how they did it, but the first two servants doubled the money they were given.

In contrast, the third servant, out of fear, buried his master's money in the ground so he wouldn't lose it.

Upon the master's return, the first two servants are praised for their willingness to take a risk in order to bring about a return. Their master said to each of them, "Well done, good and faithful servant! You have been faithful with a few things; I will put you in charge of many things. Come and share your master's happiness" (Matthew 25:21)!

When the third servant returned the single coin that belonged to his master, the man said to him:

'You wicked, lazy servant! So you knew that I harvest where I have not sown and gather where I have not scattered seed? Well then, you should have put my money on deposit with the bankers, so that when I returned I would have received it back with interest.

"So take the bag of gold from him and give it to the one who has ten bags. For whoever has will be given more, and they will have an abundance. Whoever does not have, even what they have will be taken from them. And throw that worthless servant outside, into the darkness, where there will be weeping and gnashing of teeth." (Matthew 25:26-30)

God has invested his very life in us. He expects us to do something with it. Remember what Galatians 5:1 says? "It is for freedom that Christ has set us free."

In Matthew 16:27, Jesus said, one day, He will "come in his Father's glory with his angels, and then he will reward each person according to what he has done."

God didn't deposit His Spirit into us so we would be afraid to use it. The King of the universe has shared with us His authority and power that we may continue His reign.

I think it is important to note that the servants are not praised for their ability to create a return. It's not their wise investment skills the master is pleased with, but their willingness to be faithful and take a risk.

I love the fact that some versions of this story use the term "talents" when talking about the type of money given to the servants. I like to sometimes read this story and insert our modern day meaning for the word talents: skills and abilities. God has created you in a unique way, but if you choose not to live as the one-of-a-kind person God created you to be, you deny the world the ability to see the unique expression of God that only you can reflect. You have been given a very specific set of skills and talents that, when combined with your life experiences, God will use to create a role in His Story only you can fulfill.

***

The world has yet to see what God can do with a man fully consecrated to him. By God's help, I aim to be that man.—Dwight L. Moody

In his book *Die Empty: Unleash Your Best Work Every Day*, Todd Henry talks about a word I mentioned at the beginning of this chapter: mediocre. The word mediocre comes from two Latin words: *medius*, which means middle, and *ocris*, which means rugged mountain. Henry explains that if we look at the origins of the word, it conjures up images that are much more intense than we might normally think. Rather than just meaning ordinary or moderate, mediocre literally means to give up or stop halfway up the rugged mountain.[1]

Each of us has been created with a unique purpose only we can fulfill. You were made for more. That purpose—your life's mission you might say—is a mountain, and God is calling you to the top. Just look at some of God's most radical followers in the Bible.

It was on the top of a mountain that Moses first heard God speak, announcing that he would be the leader of God's people. It was on this same mountaintop where God later gave Moses the Ten Commandments: the law that revealed our need for a savior.

It was high on a mountain where God asked Abraham to sacrifice his one and only son. Because Abraham was faithful and committed, God spared Isaac and fulfilled his promise to make Abraham the father of all nations.

It was on top of Mount Carmel that Elijah proved to the prophets of Baal the power and existence of the one, true God.

It was because of Noah's faith and obedience that he and his family were rescued from the floodwaters in the ark and landed safely atop the mountains of Ararat.

It was upon a high mountain where Peter, James, and John witnessed the miracle of their Lord, Jesus, being transfigured before their very eyes in the revealing of His divinity.

---

1. Henry, Todd. *Die Empty: Unleash Your Best Work Every Day*. New York, NY: Portfolio/Penguin, 2013.

And it was there upon a very different mountaintop, the hill of Golgotha, that Jesus Himself changed the world forever.

We can't imagine what history would be like if even one of these individuals decided to ignore God's call and stop halfway up the mountain, for it is on the tops of mountains that the world is changed.

Jesus said to His disciples,

> Truly I tell you, if you have faith as small as a mustard seed, you can say to this mountain, "Move from here to there," and it will move. Nothing will be impossible for you. (Matthew 17:20)

God has a calling for your life. What exactly that is I can't tell you. That is between you and God, but I can tell you this: it's going to require faith. It's going to be risky. It's probably not going to make a whole lot of sense, *but because God said so, you'd better do it.* This world needs you. We need the unique contribution you were created to make. There is a mountain only you can climb, a difference only you can make, a chapter only you can write, and a place among the temple wall that only you can fill.

God has a plan and a purpose for your life. It probably doesn't look anything like you might expect. I sure wasn't planning on becoming a writer and speaker. Here's the really cool part, though. When we delight ourselves in God, meaning we take great joy in seeking Him and following Him, that is when He gives us the desires of our hearts. It doesn't necessarily mean that He gives us the things *we* want, but He places longings into our hearts. The desires that come from God are always the desires of God, and when we have yearnings that align with God's, those are the ones He seeks to fulfill.[+]

I never thought I would be excited to wake up every morning and write, but there is something magical that happens when I know I am in the will of God. There is a peace, contentedness, and sense of fulfillment that comes when you are operating in your calling. There is no feeling quite like the one that accompanies the knowledge that you are right where God wants you, and He is working alongside you. It is anything but boring, average, or mediocre. It is radical. It is set-apart. It's the adventurous life we were made to live and the story we were made to tell. It's God's Story. It's a story of a people who abandoned their God, but because of His great love, He never abandoned them. He set them free that they might escape and embrace a radical, set-apart life right back where they belong.[+]

+ Waiting on God to fulfill His purpose in our life is hard. Read more on page 44 of the complimentary guide *Plan Your ESCAPE*. Discussion questions for this chapter can be found on page 46. You can download the guide for FREE at HeatherRaeHutzel.com/PlanYourEscape

CHAPTER 14

REFINE

[ri-fahyn]
verb

1. to bring to a fine or a pure state; free from
impurities:
*"Like a piece of gold, his character was being
refined."*

I t was the week after Easter, and I was stuck. I
hadn't touched this book or written a single word
for two solid months. I knew it was time to start
writing again, but I couldn't remember where I left
off, and I had no idea where to start.

God must have seen my plight because, as He's
done time and time again, He gave me an answer.

Not so unlike the times before, the answer came in the form of one, simple word.

I met a friend for brunch that week. Little did I know, God would use her words to give me my answer. Our conversation that morning would ultimately become the turning point and transformational moment for the message of this book.

As soon as we arrived at the restaurant and sat down at our table, my friend said to me, "Hey, I think God gave me a word for you."

Now to some, this conversation might seem strange, but I've learned, no matter how strange it might feel, it's always good to listen when you think God is speaking.

Not sure what to expect, I replied, "Really? Alright, well let's hear it."

"Well, it's actually two words," she said, "and the first word is 'escape.'"

I stared at her blankly, knowing she had no idea what significance that word held for me. She was completely oblivious to the fact that I was writing another book, and she certainly had no idea that the word 'escape' was the title.

I paused as I let her words sink in. Then without any other explanation I said, "The title of the book I'm writing is *Escape*."

"You're kidding?!" she asked incredulously.

I shook my head.

She was floored. "Wow, that's incredible! Here's the thing, though." She continued, "The strange part is the way God gave me the word."

"How did it happen?" I asked her.

"You're going to think this is so weird."

I chuckled, "Trust me, it can't be too weird. I've seen plenty of crazy things when it comes to God. Nothing is too strange anymore." (Famous last words.)

"Well, okay," she continued. "On my way here to brunch, I was stopped at a stop sign..."

I held up my hand, signaling her to pause, "Wait." (The beginning of her story was sounding a little too familiar.) "I already know what you're going to say," I interjected.

"You do?"

I nodded. "Yes, but go on."

"Well, I was stopped at a stop sign," she continued, "and the car in front of me was a Ford Escape. The word 'escape' leapt out at me. I don't know why, but I felt like it was a message from God for you."

I'm telling you, friend, these are the kinds of crazy, radical things that happen once we have escaped the Story of the World and begin to embrace the set-apart life God has for us. We get to live and witness miracles and experience the power of God as He originally planned.

I proceeded to tell my friend how, just the year before, God gave me the exact same word using the exact same delivery method. We were both completely blown away.

After taking a few minutes to process the awesomeness of God, our conversation continued. My friend went on to tell me the second word God gave her.

For me, the first word, "escape," was a confirmation from God. It was Him letting me know, "Yes, you did hear Me right. This is definitely the book you are supposed to be writing."

The second word was different. This word would become the guiding lamp, illuminating the direction and path of this entire book. It, too, was a word God had given me before, yet it was one I had long ago forgotten. As my friend spoke the word to me, it resurfaced from my memory with new clarity and meaning. It was a word filled with hope and promise, but it also contained a warning and sense of urgency.

"The second word," she told me, "is fire."

***

See to it that you do not refuse him who speaks. If they did not escape when they refused him who warned them on earth, how much less will we, if we turn away from him who warns us from heaven? At that time his voice shook the earth, but now he has promised, "Once more I will shake not only the earth but also the heavens." The words "once more" indicate the removing of what can be shaken—that is, created things—so that what cannot be shaken may remain.

Therefore, since we are receiving a kingdom that cannot be shaken, let us be thankful, and so worship God acceptably with reverence and awe, for our "God is a consuming fire." (Hebrews 12:25-29)

What comes to mind when you hear the word "fire?" Do you picture warm, amber flames safely confined within the ring of a fire pit, dancing wildly in the midst of a dark, summer night? Or do you imagine painful, daunting flames that reach out like a raging forest fire, consuming and destroying everything in its path?

Fire is neither good nor bad; it's a neutral element. Whether or not it is beneficial or damaging is determined by the perspective of the one in its presence. So too with God.

The Bible's depiction of God as a consuming fire is an illustration of God's holiness. As we know, only things that are holy can exist in the presence of Yahweh. Anything that is not holy is ultimately destroyed in His presence. This is why Jesus had to take on our sin and unholiness. In order for us to be one with God and stand in His presence, we had to be like God.

In the beginning, God created humanity to be holy both in a physical and spiritual form, but that came to a rather quick end when Adam and Eve sinned against God. Jesus came to make a way back for us and reverse the damnation we brought upon ourselves.

In a spiritual sense, God has been able to redeem us. He destroyed our sin through the death of Jesus on the cross, and by taking on our unholiness, He made us holy and blameless.

Though our sins have been forgiven and made obsolete, clearly, we as human beings continue to do things that are considered sinful. While the trueness of our identity and character is complete in the spiritual realm, it is not yet fully manifested in our physical realm.

2 Corinthians 3:18 says we are "being transformed into his image with ever-increasing glory." That transformation comes as a result of the work of the Holy Spirit inside us. While God Himself is the one who completes this work in us, we do have a role to play.

Our job is to be yielded to the Spirit in order to experience our full transformation. It is the Holy Spirit, God within us, who leads us in His Story. His still small voice is the gentle prodding of the author and director, leading and guiding us through the pages. He forms and develops our character while pointing us toward the final chapter of the story, where we will be revealed for who we truly are. This is the moment when we stand before the consuming, fiery presence of our God. His refining holiness will reveal what we have become.

A fire is the perfect illustration of what we will experience on the day we stand before the holy presence of God. When placed inside a fire, some materials are destroyed while others are able to withstand the flames. It all depends on what an item is made of as to whether or not it will remain or be consumed.

When thrown into a fire, materials like grass, straw, and hay are completely burned up, but other more precious substances, such as gold, are actually made more perfect when they pass through the flames. Consider for a moment the way gold is purified.

When a goldsmith works with a piece of gold, he has to first refine or perfect it. In its natural state, gold is full of all kinds of impurities and blemishes. The way the goldsmith removes those unwanted pieces is by heating up the gold in a fire. In the heat of a fire, the gold melts and all of the impurities rise to the surface. They are either burned away in the flames or scraped off by the goldsmith. This process is the only way for the goldsmith to remove the undesirable parts. It takes the metal worker several rounds of heating, filtering, cooling, and scraping, but eventually the gold is refined into a pure state.

Now imagine that you are a piece of gold. Going through the process of refining isn't damaging; it actually makes the gold better. But if you, the gold, have lots of impurities, the process might feel painful. You're being heated up and melted down. Parts of you are being scraped off and removed. It hurts to go through the fire, but on the other side you will emerge perfected.

While we do go through a sort of purifying process here on earth, it's not the same as the refining we will experience one day in the future. Here on earth, the Holy Spirit is working in and through us to create a return on the investment God has placed inside us. He breaks and chips away the pieces of us that don't look like the end result: the image of God. At the same time, He multiplies Himself in us until we look less like our sinful selves and more like His holy presence.

Galatians 5 talks about the fruit of the Spirit as an indicator of this transformation process. "The fruit of the Spirit is love, joy, peace, forbearance, kindness, goodness, faithfulness, gentleness and self-control" (Galatians 5:22-23).

The fruit of the Spirit is called that for a reason; it is the product of someone being completely and utterly filled with the Spirit of God to the point of overflowing. It's not the fruit of our trying harder. It's not the fruit of our attempting to be a better or more loving person. On our own, we cannot produce genuine, spiritual fruit. We can manufacture a disingenuous version of these character qualities, but we cannot create real fruit. It is only as a result of the Holy Spirit living deep within us and living through us that we can actually reflect God's image. Transformation comes only as a result of us being yielded to the work of the Holy Spirit within us. We can't do it on our own.

John 15:1-4 says:

I am the true vine, and my Father is the gardener. He cuts off every branch in me that bears no fruit, while every branch that does bear fruit he prunes so that it will be even more fruitful. You are already clean because of the word I have spoken to you. Remain in me, as I also remain in you. No branch can bear fruit by itself; it must remain in the vine. Neither can you bear fruit unless you remain in me.

Here on earth, we may be able to live what seems like a "righteous" life, but the proof is in the fruit. We can be a people who produce artificial, manufactured versions of a Spirit-filled life, becoming nothing more than a pretty bowl of plastic grapes, but God knows the real thing. The authenticity of the fruit is revealed by the root.

John the Baptist was another one of God's servants who preached a message of repentance, and He said it this way: "The ax is already at the root of the trees, and every tree that does not produce good fruit will be cut down and thrown into the fire" (Matthew 3:10).

Jesus Himself said that His true followers are recognized by their fruit. In Matthew 7:16-20 He says:

Do people pick grapes from thornbushes, or figs from thistles? Likewise, every good tree bears good fruit, but a bad tree bears bad fruit. A good tree cannot bear bad fruit, and a bad tree cannot bear good fruit. Every tree that does not bear good fruit is cut down and thrown into the fire. Thus, by their fruit you will recognize them.

In ancient times, when a harvest was completed, anything that was not consistent with the harvest or fruitful was burned and destroyed. It will be the same way with us. It is in the refining fires of God's all-consuming presence that we are exposed for what we are. Here on earth, we are a work in progress, but one day, we will stand before the Almighty King on the Day of Judgement.

The judgment or wrath of God is not what we would normally think when we conjure up images of these words in our minds. God's judgment, wrath, or fiery presence is simply His holiness. If we have allowed Him to transform us into His holy image, then His purifying presence will perfect us. If we have not escaped and have not made ourselves one with God, we will be consumed. It is the nature of God's holiness. Remember, it is not God's desire to destroy us; it is the natural consequence of being an unholy being in the presence of a holy God. God made a way for us to come back to Him, but have we accepted it?

The awaited day when Jesus returns has often been called The Great and Terrible Day because for some this day will be terrible, but for others this day will be great.

In the Gospel of Matthew, Jesus said:

Not everyone who says to me, 'Lord, Lord,' will enter the kingdom of heaven, but only the one who does the will of my Father who is in heaven. Many will say to me on that day, 'Lord, Lord, did we not prophesy in your name and in your name drive out demons and in your name perform many miracles?' Then I will tell them plainly, 'I never knew you. Away from me, you evildoers!' (Matthew 7:21-23)

The will of God is this: for us to know Him and to be like Him so we can make Him known, that is, to know His true character in order to be transformed into it.

It is immediately after Jesus gives this warning in Matthew 7:21-23 that He goes on to share the story of the wise and foolish builder. Jesus follows His caution with this story and teaching in order to reveal that, without Jesus as our foundation, we will never be transformed into beings who are able to withstand the flames.

Just like a fire, it is the position and perspective of those in God's presence that determine how they perceive God. Those who are yielded to God and have the Holy Spirit living inside of them have been made holy as God is holy. These people are congruent with Jesus. They are made of His Spirit, and that Spirit can stand blameless before our God.

While the pieces of us that don't look like Jesus will be burned away, the parts of us that have been transformed will be revealed. The question we have to ask ourselves is this: after we pass through the fiery flame of God's presence, what will be left of us?

The more we allow ourselves to be transformed during our time on earth, the more like God we will be when we stand before Him. We do not have to be perfect when we die. None of us are perfect, nor can we be perfect here on earth. We will all be refined to some degree. The question is, how much of us will be left when Jesus comes back for us? Will we, like the good and faithful servants in the parable of the talents, say to our Master, "See! We have multiplied your inheritance!" Or will we be like the other servant who simply returned what was owed to the Master?

Jesus will return for the deposit of His Spirit. How much of you will He take with Him? 1 Corinthians 3:10-15 says:

> By the grace God has given me, I laid a foundation as a wise builder, and someone else is building on it. But each one should build with care. For no one can lay any foundation other than the one already laid, which is Jesus Christ. If anyone builds on this foundation using gold, silver, costly stones, wood, hay or straw, their work will be shown for what it is, because the Day will bring it to light. It will be revealed with fire, and the fire will test the quality of each person's work. If what has been built survives, the builder will receive a reward. If it is burned up, the builder will suffer loss but yet will be saved—even though only as one escaping through the flames.

With what materials are we building the temple of God, the Church? Are we building with people who reflect the image of God? People who are gold, silver, and costly stones? Or are God's people made merely of wood, hay and straw?

Who are you? Are you yielded to the transformative work of the Spirit in your life? Are you embracing the set-apart life God has given you in His Story? Are you living in the Kingdom of

God? Are you allowing Him to chip and chisel away at you to reveal the image hiding underneath?

***

When a goldsmith is in the process of refining a precious metal, there is only one way for him to know when the gold is ready and the refining is finished. The metal has been made pure when he can see his own reflection in the surface of the gold.

God's image is inside you. It's who you were made to be, but God doesn't want to wait until the end of the age to reveal that image. He wants to reveal it now through the transformative work of His Spirit.

God gives us a choice in this matter. We can choose to be refined now or consumed later. We decide just how much of ourselves is conformed to the image of God. We get to decide whether or not we will have anything left to escape the consuming fire of His all holy presence.

In chapter 7, we described hell as a prison locked from the inside. It's true. The presence of God is Heaven for those of us who have made ourselves one with Him. Because we are holy as He is holy, His presence is an overwhelming, warm, and euphoric experience. But for those who reject God—who refuse to make themselves one with Him and cling to unholiness—for them, the presence of God is hell. They experience Him as an all-consuming lake of fire.

We will all enter into the presence of God at the end of the age. What will be your experience of God? Heaven or hell?

***

God is in the process of not just refining humanity, but refining all of creation. "For God so loved *the world*," that's why He sent Jesus (John 3:16). Just as we have a choice in our own transformation process, we also have a role to play in the transformation of creation. It's up to us as to whether or not we build things now that will last for eternity.

Romans 8:19-21 says:

> The creation waits in eager expectation for the children of God to be revealed. For the creation was subjected to frustration, not by its own choice, but by the will of the one who subjected it, in hope that the creation itself will be liberated from its bondage to decay and brought into the freedom and glory of the children of God. We know that the whole creation has been groaning as in the pains of childbirth right up to the present time.

Creation groans as it waits for us to realize who we are created to be—the Sons of God—and what we are supposed to do—reign with His character of love, committing everything in existence to His Kingdom. God doesn't want us to wait for physical death to start living the life He designed for us. If we have the Spirit of the living God inside us, we are already eternal beings. We can start rebuilding our eternal Kingdom here and now!

So let us ask ourselves these very important questions: what are we building in our lives? What type of relationships are we building? What kinds of families are we establishing? What sort of businesses and ministries are we creating? Are our finances being used to create Kingdom value? Are our lives leaving an indelible fingerprint on this earth, one that cannot be erased by wind, rain, or fire? What materials are we using to build our lives? Are we building with hay, straw, and grass? Or are we building with gold, silver, and precious stones? Are we looking to our foundation and building upon the solid cornerstone Jesus Christ?

Sweet Church, when Jesus returns, what will He find here? Will we have completed our task of continuing His work as the Body of Christ?

When Jesus last visited us He said, "The Kingdom of God is at hand."

Dear reader, the Kingdom of God is here! It's right here and right now! I've said it before; we aren't building the Kingdom from scratch. Rather, we are seeking it. We are searching for it amongst the rubble, unearthing and rebuilding it.

Jesus instructed us to pray, "Father, let your Kingdom come and let your will be done on earth as it is in Heaven" (Matthew 6:10). These are not just words to be recited; we are to live our lives according to this prayer.

While it has been over 2,000 years, and we don't know when the exact day will come, Jesus promised His return. Heaven is not some far off location. Heaven—the presence of God—will come to earth, and in the presence of His all-consuming holiness, the earth and all its inhabitants will be refined by fire and exposed for what they are.

2 Peter 3 says:

> Above all, you must understand that in the last days scoffers will come, scoffing and following their own evil desires. They will say, "Where is this 'coming' he promised? Ever since our ancestors died, everything goes on as it has since the beginning of creation." But they deliberately forget that long ago by God's word the heavens came into being and the earth was formed out of water and by water. By these waters also the world of that time was deluged and destroyed. By the same word the present heavens and earth are reserved for fire, being kept for the day of judgment and destruction of the ungodly.
>
> But do not forget this one thing, dear friends: With the Lord a day is like a thousand years, and a thousand years are like a day. The Lord is not slow in keeping his promise, as some understand slowness. Instead he is patient with you, not wanting anyone to perish, but everyone to come to repentance.

But the day of the Lord will come like a thief. The heavens will disappear with a roar; the elements will be destroyed by fire, and the earth and everything done in it will be laid bare.

Since everything will be destroyed in this way, what kind of people ought you to be? You ought to live holy and godly lives as you look forward to the day of God and speed its coming. That day will bring about the destruction of the heavens by fire, and the elements will melt in the heat. But in keeping with his promise we are looking forward to a new heaven and a new earth, where righteousness dwells. (verses 3-13)

God is patient. He wants all to come to repentance and turn away from sin. He wants everyone to escape!

Sweet friend, it is time. It is time to escape the Story of the World and embrace the radical, set-apart life God designed for us to live in *His* Story. God is calling each of us to fulfill our purpose as His image bearers, so that:

The body of Christ may be built up until we all reach unity in the faith and in the knowledge of the Son of God and become mature, attaining to the whole measure of the fullness of Christ. (Ephesians 4:12-13)

I've said it before, and I'll say it again—we are in the final chapter of this story. We have a role to play. When we participate in God's Story, living out our God ordained role as His image bearers, we hasten His coming.

Just like we see God doing in Genesis 1, we have the power to create order out of chaos. This has been our mandate since the very beginning of creation.

In Genesis 1:28, God instructed us to be fruitful and multiply, not just for the sake of procreation, but for the sake of subduing the earth and expanding His dominion.

While we may have lost this authority and power through the sinfulness of mankind, Jesus came to restore it. Because we have been made one with Him, our identity and rights have been re-established. Jesus re-commissioned us with our original role as human beings right before He ascended into Heaven. Here is what He said to His followers:

> All authority in heaven and on earth has been given to me. Therefore go and make disciples of all nations, baptizing them in the name of the Father and of the Son and of the Holy Spirit, and teaching them to obey everything I have commanded you. And surely I am with you always, to the very end of the age. (Matthew 28:18-20)

Sweet friend, the Kingdom of God started with Jesus, but it didn't end with Him. It continues with us! The Kingdom of God breaks through when one little stone allows itself to be shaped to perfection, committing to serve its purpose among a greater piece of work, the temple of God. Not a physical building but something wonderful and entirely different, and that temple, the gathering of God's people, becomes the starting point for building something even more amazing—the Kingdom of God.

In Revelation 21:22, John says this about His vision of the coming Heaven: "I did not see a temple in the city, because the Lord God Almighty and the Lamb are its temple."

At the end of days, we will experience our oneness with God in full. We can't understand it now. It's a mystery as Paul says in Ephesians 5:22, a mystery that He equates to the relationship between a husband and wife. While we can't fully comprehend it, we know that when the refining presence of God comes to earth, what will be left is what was rebuilt upon the foundation of Jesus.

What will Christ find when He returns? Will we be ready? After we are refined, what will be revealed? Will we be prepared like a beautifully adorned bride waiting for her groom, or as 1 Corinthians 3:15 says, will we barely manage to escape through the fire?+

+ For discussion questions for this chapter, check out page 47 in the complimentary guide *Plan Your ESCAPE*. You can download it for FREE at HeatherRaeHutzel.com/PlanYourEscape

CHAPTER 15

UNVEIL

[uhn-veyl]
verb

1. to reveal or disclose by or as if by removing a
veil or covering:
*"Finally, on the last page of the book, the mystery
was unveiled."*

Throughout history, humans have tried to understand and explain the story of God's love for us. It's a mystery that haunts humanity. Artists have painted murals, authors have written books, and directors have created movies, but none of these have come close to encapsulating the enigmatic nature of God. Even my own feeble attempts with this book will fall utterly short in comparison to the greatness of the force of His love.

While mankind has sought to know and understand our relationship with God, we have often overlooked the very tools the Almighty has given us. The Bible uses many analogies to describe and explain the spiritual truths in God's Story. For example, the Bible tells us God is a loving Father; it also describes Him as a sacrificial husband, a friend, and even in places, likens Him to a mother. So what is God? Is He a Father, a husband, a friend, or a mother? The answer is, "Yes." He is all of these things and more because each encompasses a different aspect of the love that He is. The truth of God's identity is so far outside our realm of understanding, but He is gracious enough to give us multiple analogies to help us understand and relate to Him. No one analogy can fully encompass God's identity, but they can help us to understand certain aspects of it.

Although God gives us beautiful analogies and symbolism in His Word to help us grasp the things human words cannot describe, these comparisons all break down at some point. It is when we, in our humanity, corrupt and dilute the very words and parallels God uses that His analogies become utterly void of the meaning and beauty they once captured. Like when a father abuses his child, or when a husband cheats on his wife, or when our friends only like us because of what we can do for them, or when our mother gives us gifts with strings attached. When we use the analogies God has given us, we must always view them in light of the perfect and original story of God, before the sin of humans entered the world.

While the Bible uses many different comparisons to explain God's love and relationship with us, there is one that best illustrates the story He is telling—the relationship between a groom and his bride.

Throughout the Bible, the story of the bride and bridegroom is used to illustrate the relationship between Jesus Christ and the Church body at large. While a perfect depiction of this analogy would be one faithful man committed to one faithful woman, both equally and sacrificially serving one another in love, what we see in the Bible is completely different.

The Bible makes it clear that this perfect relationship is God's ideal not just for our earthly marriages but also our heavenly marriage to Him. Yet because of our fallen nature, we are not the faithful, committed bride who is willing to sacrifice for her groom. We, as the Church, are an adulterous bride.

Nowhere is this more clearly illustrated in the Bible than in the book of Hosea. In this small chapter of God's Story, Hosea, a prophet, is told by God to marry a promiscuous woman. So Hosea married a woman named Gomer, who was most likely a shrine prostitute at a temple to a foreign god. Perhaps not so surprisingly, Gomer "runs around" on her husband and ends up being sold into slavery. Listen to what God says to Hosea. "Go, show your love to your wife again, though she is loved by another man and is an adulteress. Love her as the Lord loves the Israelites, though they turn to other gods" (Hosea 3:1).

So Hosea purchased back his bride.

The entire book of Hosea is a beautiful picture of how, despite the fact that we, the Bride of Christ, take our eyes off our Bridegroom and choose the Story of the World, He still loves us.

While God created marriage as a sacred covenant to represent the beautiful relationship between God and humans, we redefined the meaning of that covenant. I'm not just talking about the controversial discussions surrounding marriage in our culture today. Marriage was redefined the moment sin entered the world. Marriage was redefined the moment Adam blamed Eve for his folly. Marriage was redefined the moment husbands began treating their wives as property. Marriage was redefined the first time a woman deceived her husband. Marriage was redefined the moment sex took place outside of the established covenant. Marriage was redefined the first time a wife had an affair. Marriage was redefined the first time a husband beat his bride. And marriage was redefined the first time a couple, who promised each other forever, severed the bond that made them one.

Despite our ability to degrade the sacred institution of earthly marriage, perhaps our greatest blunder of all is the way we've debased our heavenly marriage. But our God is so ridiculously good, and He is still the author of our story, and here is how HE defines marriage: "This is how we know what love is: Jesus Christ laid down his life for us. And we ought to lay down our lives for our brothers and sisters" (1 John 3:16).

God defines marriage in saying, "While you were still sinners, I died for you" (Romans 5:8).

God defines marriage by saying, "If hell is where you are, then that is where I will go. I said, 'Forever.' I said, 'For better, for worse, for richer, for poorer, in sickness and in health, that even death may never keep us apart!' I said, 'As long as we both shall live;' therefore, I extend to you the gift of eternal life!"

The book of Hosea may be the most obvious depiction of the bride and bridegroom relationship, but it's most certainly not the only one. In fact, the husband/wife relationship is held up as the ultimate analogy of God's relationship to us, and is, therefore, scattered throughout the story of the Bible. However, you may be surprised where you will find it.

One of the unique things about the Bible in comparison to any other ancient Near Eastern piece of literature is the way it addresses women. During the time in which the Bible was penned, women were viewed and treated very poorly. To the men of those days, women were pieces of property, but the Bible does something unique: the Bible tells the stories of women. There is a very important reason why: the women in the Bible tell the story of the Bride.

In his book, *The Coming Bride*, Pastor David Jones illustrates how each and every woman in the Bible represents and depicts the Bride of Christ in some way, shape, or form. Jones says:

The story of the Bride is perhaps the greatest mystery in the Bible. It is God's parable and revelation of the relationship between Jesus and His Church... The story of the woman is the hidden yet most desired entity in God's redemption strategy... Much has been written and preached concerning the men in the Bible, but the essential presence of the woman is often overlooked. Jesus, however, never overlooked any woman in His creation, as He understood that they were a beautiful picture of the Church: His Bride. These women represent the Bride that He came to save; the Church that He loves and is coming back for.[1]

Jones proceeds to go through the Bible and highlight the stories of various women: from Eve to Sarah, Rebekah to Rachel, Ruth to Bathsheba, and Esther to Mary the mother of Jesus. Each and every woman's story paints a picture of the Bride of Christ, sometimes negatively, sometimes positively.

Let's take a quick look at one of these women, the very first woman God created. She was the perfect embodiment of Christ's Bride. Her name was Eve.

While both men and women are to represent the Church, and both genders are also to reflect Jesus Christ, there are ways in which a woman can represent the Bride that a man cannot, and similarly, there are ways in which a man can represent Jesus

---

1. Jones, David. *The Coming Bride*. Trywalla Publications, 2014.

Christ that a woman cannot. Based on the sheer fact that, in a marriage relationship, the man is the bridegroom and a woman is the bride, these gender differences tell the story of God's relationship to us.

In the story of Adam and Eve, Adam is the Christ figure, and Eve represents the Bride: the Church. Jones says it this way in his book:

> God begins the divine narrative by describing the unique creation of a bride for, "Adam, the Son of God." Just as "Adam... was a pattern of the one to come," so Eve is a pattern of the Church that is to come.

The symbolism is seemingly endless when it comes to the relationship between Adam and Eve. The very manner in which Eve is created is so telling.

Genesis 2:21-23 says,

> So the Lord God caused the man to fall into a deep sleep; and while he was sleeping, he took one of the man's ribs and then closed up the place with flesh. Then the Lord God made a woman from the rib he had taken out of the man, and he brought her to the man.
> The man said,
> "This is now bone of my bones
>   and flesh of my flesh;
> she shall be called 'woman,'
>   for she was taken out of man."

The beauty of what we see taking place here is this: in the same way that the life of Adam was suspended in order for his bride, Eve, to be created and given life, so too, our Bridegroom Jesus had His life suspended for us. Jones goes on to say:

"Without this sacrifice being made there was no possibility that anyone could ever belong to God. Jesus had to die in order for His Bride to live and He was willing to give up His life for her."

Backing up a couple verses, we see something even more significant: the reason for the creation of the Bride.

The Lord God said, "It is not good for the man to be alone. I will make a helper suitable for him."
Now the Lord God had formed out of the ground all the wild animals and all the birds in the sky. He brought them to the man to see what he would name them; and whatever the man called each living creature, that was its name. So the man gave names to all the livestock, the birds in the sky and all the wild animals. But for Adam no suitable helper was found. (Genesis 2:18-20)

In chapter 4, we said God needs us. Not that He, in some way, is sustained by our existence or dependent on us, but "need" in the sense that we might say to our spouse, "I need you in my life. I don't want to be without you."

In the same way that Adam was in need of relational companionship, God was in need of relationship. After all, God is a relational being. God is love. So what did God do? He created human beings.

In the creation account in Genesis, after everything He made, God said, "This is good." There is only one thing that He declared as "not good," and that was for the man to be alone.

Eve, the woman, the depiction of the Bride, was the final piece of creation. She was the crowning gem of all God had made. And what did He say after creating her lovely form and bringing her before her groom? "This is *very* good!"

Can't you just imagine God dusting off His hands saying, "I'm done! That's it. It's perfect! Now, I can rest." Because what did God do next? He rested on the seventh day, the Sabbath.

So too, one day, when this world comes to an end and the Church of God is finished and complete, the Bride will stand before her Groom, and He will say, "I'm done! That's it. It's perfect! Now, I can rest. It's time for eternal Sabbath!"

However, like Eve with the serpent, we too have been deceived and gone astray. We are still in the process of being formed on our journey of escape. We are being transformed into His image with ever increasing glory. Here's where the story gets really good.

In chapter 3, I told you that when I first began my journey, God was constantly prompting me to read from the books of Genesis and Revelation in the Bible. Now, we've already talked about Eve in Genesis. Genesis is the beginning, the first chapter of the Bible. The word Genesis literally means "beginning." But it's not God's beginning—*it's our beginning.*

God's story is uniquely marked by the fact that His intention was *not* to chronicle His greatness and awesomeness as an all-powerful deity. Yes, of course we see God's majesty in the Bible, but that was not the story God recorded. Instead, the story God tells is the story of His great love for us—the Story of the Bride. From the very beginning of the Bible, God makes a bold declaration about who He is, who we are, and what kind of story He is telling.

But God was pointing me in the direction of two books: Genesis and Revelation. Revelation is the last book of the Bible, but the word "revelation" doesn't mean ending; it means "to reveal," "to make something known." Quite literally it means "*to unveil.*" While Genesis is the creation of the Bride, Revelation is the unveiling of the Bride. This is why the "end times" are often called the Apocalypse. The word "apocalypse" has the same meaning as the word "revelation." The Apocalypse will be a time of disclosure. It is the moment when God reveals who we truly are.

In 1 John chapter 3 it says:

Dear friends, now we are children of God, and what we will be has not yet been made known. But we know that when Christ appears, we shall be like Him, for we shall

220

see Him as He is. All who have this hope in Him purify themselves, just as He is pure. (verses 2-3)

God is chipping and chiseling away at us to reveal the image hiding underneath, an image that looks just like Him. We don't know exactly what we will look like or be like as the Bride of Christ, but we know it will be something precious, radical, and oh so set-apart. We will be completed and perfected on the day Jesus returns. Jesus Himself will lift our veil.

We already know, at the end of days God will refine the earth by fire in the same way that the earth was once refined by the great flood of Noah. God will reveal His Bride in fullness one day, but His true desire is to reveal her *now*. He wants His Bride to know who she is, her true identity: an image-bearer of God, a holy nation, a royal priesthood, a Son of God, *the Bride of Christ*.

God wants us to realize now and live now like we were made for more because we most certainly have been. God is calling out to us. He is shouting, "Behold! The Kingdom of God has come near. The Story of God is being written right now. You can live the life you were made for now. I designed you for this story. You were made for it. It's right here waiting for you. Repent! Turn away from your old story and your old way of life. Escape! Break free from the Story of the World, and live as though you truly have escaped. You are free! Believe that it is true because it is. Embrace a radical, set-apart life. I tell you the truth: you were made for this story. This, My beloved, is the good news!"

Jesus is calling us to fulfill our role in His Story and reveal to the world the trueness of who we were always meant to be from the beginning of creation—the Bride of the King of the Universe.

While all this is true, sweet Church, let me ask again, "What will Jesus find when He returns?"

I hear the Spirit of God saying, "I am coming soon, but My Bride is not ready yet."

It's time to make ourselves ready. It's time to prepare for our Groom. We need to allow Him to shape us into the people we were always meant to be. That way, when Jesus comes to lift our veil, what is revealed is the precious, all Holy Bride of Christ.

As the Bride of our King, we have a responsibility to reveal this great story to others. Let's take a quick look at one final woman in the Bible: Mary Magdalene.

Mary was one of Jesus' many followers, but there is something very significant about Mary: she was the first person to arrive at the tomb after Jesus rose from the grave. The woman, the Bride, was the first one to know that her Groom was alive. She was the one to run back and tell the world the good news, "He is risen! He is alive! And not only is He alive, but He is coming soon!"

As the Bride of the King of the Universe, it is our own personal duty to make Him known. Just as Mary Magdalene once did, we are to run back and tell the others, "The stone has been rolled away from the tomb and put into place as the cornerstone! Our King is alive, and He is coming soon!"

***

In the book of Revelation, the Apostle John describes his vision of the end times. Listen to what he says in chapter 21:

One of the seven angels who had the seven bowls full of the seven last plagues came and said to me, "Come, I will show you the bride, the wife of the Lamb." And he carried me away in the Spirit to a mountain great and high, and showed me the Holy City, Jerusalem, coming down out of heaven from God. It shone with the glory of God, and its brilliance was like that of a very precious jewel... (verses 9-11)

The temple of God is not to be made out of just any type of stone but precious stone, stones that are radically beautiful and set-apart, crowning gems.

I will rebuild you with stones of turquoise,
    your foundations with lapis lazuli.
I will make your battlements of rubies,
    your gates of sparkling jewels,
    and all your walls of precious stones.
(Isaiah 54:11-12)

While each and every one of us has a unique role to play in God's Story, we are all called to know Him, to be like Him, and to make Him known. Jesus is seeking the lost stones for His temple, and He is sending His Bride to gather them.

As I near the end of this book, I feel the weightiness of my own calling, my own part in His Story. The task I have been assigned is to deliver this message:

"Dear Church, we were made for more! Our Groom is coming soon, but we are not ready. It is our wedding day, but our hair is a mess, we don't have our dress on, and we haven't even bathed. We are sitting alone inside this dark, dank prison cell while the door stands wide open, our King visible on the horizon. Escape, sweet Bride. Run away as fast as you can from your old way of life, and embrace something that is radical and set-apart. Make yourself ready for Him. Yield to the Holy Spirit inside you. Allow yourself to be transformed into His image with ever increasing glory."

We were made for more than watered-down, Americanized Christianity. Heck, we were made for more than the most devoted and spiritual churches we can find on the face of the earth. We were made for Jesus. We were made for His Story!

We are His image bearers, His body, His temple. We are the Sons of God, a Holy nation, a Royal Priesthood. We are the Bride of the Living God.

Revelation 22 says:

"Look, I am coming soon! My reward is with me, and I will give to each person according to what they have done. I am the

Alpha and the Omega, the First and the Last, the Beginning and the End. "Blessed are those who wash their robes, that they may have the right to the tree of life and may go through the gates into the city.

"I, Jesus, have sent my angel to give you this testimony for the churches. I am the Root and the Offspring of David, and the bright Morning Star." The Spirit and the bride say, "Come!" And let the one who hears say, "Come!" Let the one who is thirsty come; and let the one who wishes take the free gift of the water of life. He who testifies to these things says, "Yes, I am coming soon." (verses 12-14,16-17,20)

And to that I say, "Amen! Come, Lord Jesus, come. May we be a Bride prepared for her Groom. Come, Lord Jesus, come!"[+]

CHAPTER 16

END

[end]
noun

1. termination; conclusion; the concluding part:
*"As he turned the last page he realized it was not
the end but merely the beginning."*

You, my brothers and sisters, were called to
be free. But do not use your freedom to
indulge the flesh; rather, serve one another
humbly in love. For the entire law is
fulfilled in keeping this one command:
"Love your neighbor as yourself."
(Galatians 5:13-14)

I t's hard to believe we are coming to the end of our time together in this book.[+] But make no mistake; your journey is just beginning. You now have a responsibility, friend. It is for the sake of freedom (and not just your own) that you have been set free (Galatians 5:1). The Spirit of the Lord is on you, because he has anointed you to proclaim good news to the poor. He has sent you to proclaim freedom for the prisoners and recovery of sight for the blind, to set the oppressed free and proclaim the year of the Lord's favor (Luke 4:18-19). This is your commissioning. This is your mission on this epic adventure. Jesus is sending you back to the prison compound to help the others escape. Like Neo, Morpheus, Trinity, and the other characters in *The Matrix*, you are now a freedom fighter. It won't be easy because, like the Matrix, the Story of the World cannot be seen. It is inherently deceptive, and the vast majority of the world has fallen asleep to it. The only way we can wake others from this dream is to expose them to something different— God's Story. We do this by imaging our Leader whose name is Love. Rather than living a self-serving life, we take on the appearance of a servant, just as our perfect example Jesus did.

Philippians 2:1-11 says:

Therefore if you have any encouragement from being united with Christ, if any comfort from his love, if any common

---

+ Read the journal entry I wrote after I finished writing this book. You can find it on page 49 of the complimentary guide *Plan Your ESCAPE*. You can download it for FREE at HeatherRaeHutzel.com/PlanYourEscape

sharing in the Spirit, if any tenderness and compassion, then make my joy complete by being like-minded, having the same love, being one in spirit and of one mind. Do nothing out of selfish ambition or vain conceit. Rather, in humility value others above yourselves, not looking to your own interests but each of you to the interests of the others.

In your relationships with one another, have the same mindset as Christ Jesus:

Who, being in very nature God,
    did not consider equality with God something to be used to his own advantage;
rather, he made himself nothing
    by taking the very nature of a servant,
    being made in human likeness.
And being found in appearance as a man,
    he humbled himself
    by becoming obedient to death—
        even death on a cross!
Therefore God exalted him to the highest place
    and gave him the name that is above every name,
that at the name of Jesus every knee should bow,
    in heaven and on earth and under the earth,

and every tongue acknowledge that
Jesus Christ is Lord,
    to the glory of God the Father.

We are all born into this life with equal standing—the potential to be image-bearers of the King. Whether we are humbled or exalted is determined by the way we live our life. Those who exalt themselves are humbled, and those who humble themselves are exalted (Matthew 23:12).

Jesus is our sure foundation and solid rock, and when we, simple stones in the mighty temple of God look just exactly like the foundation, that, my friend, is when we'll be recognized. That is the moment we'll be lifted up as Sons of the Most High God.

I have fallen in love with a line Mark Batterson quotes in his book *All In* which he attributes to Korczak Ziolkowski: "When your life is over, the world will ask you only one question: 'Did you do what you were supposed to do?'"

Batterson goes on to talk about this question saying, "It cannot be answered with words. It must be answered with your life."[1]

The life we are called to live is one that is radical and set-apart. What marks it as such is the extravagant, lavish, self-sacrificial love that can be found nowhere else but in the story of God. The Bible says it is this kind of crazy, Jesus-like lifestyle that makes us stand out to the world. It is the life that answers the question, "Did you do what you

---

1. Batterson, Mark. *All In: You Are One Decision Away from a Totally Different Life*. Grand Rapids, MI: Zondervan, 2013.

were supposed to do?"

Jesus said in John 13:35 that this is how the world will identify us. He said, "By this everyone will know that you are my disciples, if you love one another."

This lifestyle requires sacrifice. It isn't easy. It requires us to escape from the comforts of our own little world, where everything revolves around us, in order to embrace a new story. A story where love is the main focus and choosing to be like Jesus is the exhilarating force that drives the plot.

No matter how hard we try to achieve and live a good life by worldly standards or, worse yet, our own standards, we will fall utterly short. God's standard for success in His Story is the only one that matters, and it looks very different. It's choosing the path of most resistance because it is the one that will beat and batter and break away all of those ugly pieces that don't look like Him. Success is a life that is completely, wholeheartedly, and unabashedly dedicated to Him and the work He calls us to do: to know Him and to make Him known through our love.

"No one can serve two masters," Jesus said. "Either you will hate the one and love the other, or you will be devoted to the one and despise the other" (Matthew 6:24). If you're familiar with this verse, then you know what Jesus said next: "You cannot serve both God and money." I'd like to add a little twist to this verse—you cannot serve both God and the American Dream. You cannot live in both God's Story and the Story of the World. You cannot have one foot in the Kingdom of God and one foot in the Kingdom of the world. You must choose in which story you will live.

The good news is this: Jesus promises that when we seek first His Kingdom and His righteousness, *everything* we need will be given to us (Matthew 6:33). This is how love works! Something supernatural and magical happens when we decide to make God's Story and His love our priority. This is how the Kingdom of God expands. By reconnecting to each other in love, we are re-joining the bricks and stones. We are unearthing the pile of rubble and rebuilding the temple of God. *Love* is what makes us a chosen people, a royal priesthood, a holy nation, God's special possession (1 Peter 2:9).

As I examine the life of Jesus, I can't help but come to one conclusion. God is calling us, who claim to be followers, to a life far more radical than the one we are currently living.

Prayers for health, protection, and prosperity are good, but more so, we should be praying for God to wreck our hearts no matter the cost. Comfort and security are not promised to the man or woman who chooses to follow Jesus but rather, trouble, persecution, trials, and even earthly death.

But take heart, dear follower, because He also promises that when we die to self "here," we gain life "there." Jesus came that we may have life abundantly, life to the fullest (John 10:10). Not a house to the fullest, not a refrigerator or a bank account to the fullest, but a heart that is overflowing with love, peace, and joy no matter what our earthly circumstances. Dear follower, in this world you will have trouble. You will face difficulty. You will be uncomfortable. But take heart, for Jesus Christ the Lord and King has overcome the world, and He is worth it all.

God is calling us to live a different life, a radical, set-apart, holy kind of life. When we look at the Gospels, this fact is undeniably so. Yet somehow, so often, we, the Church, have missed it. I love the way Jen Hatmaker puts it in her book *Interrupted*:

> God is living and active, and He still invites those with ears to hear and eyes to see into the kingdom, which Jesus explained was subversive, countercultural, radical, often hidden. The kingdom refuses to play by the rules of power politics or aggression; it refuses to bully or dominate. It whispers of embarrassing grace and thrilling insubordinance, refusing to go down without fighting for mercy. It'll cost us, dear one. I hope I make that clear in the next few pages. The very comforts the American dream and American Christianity hold out to us are the same ones we must abandon without looking back, daring to trust that a Savior who had no place to lay His head might have the slightest idea what He was talking about. We must trust that He would never lead us astray, although you might find yourself questioning tenets that once held your sweet little life together. And that will hurt and people will probably criticize it and you

might cry. I know I did. But hear me: You will go out in joy and be led forth in peace; the mountains and the hills will burst into song before you, and all the trees of the field will clap their hands (Isaiah 55:12). Isaiah was right. Those trees will clap indeed. This is the stuff, good reader. This is it. We can follow our Jesus to every dark, scary, broken place He just insists on going, determined to heal and restore people, because He is a good Savior and we can trust Him. And as it turns out, as soon as we are willing to be the last, we actually become first. When we admit we are least, we feel like the greatest. And when we lose our lives, we find it all . . . all the love, all the life, all the thrill, all the fulfillment. I can't believe it. Everything Jesus ever said was true.[2]

As I continue on this journey of following my Jesus, I'm finding that my life here on earth makes less sense, and yet, at the same time, it makes more sense. The harder I try, the less I accomplish. The more I let go, the more ground I cover. The less I own, the more I have. The more painful the sacrifice, the sweeter the reward. When I *try* to be like God, I fail, but when I *let* God be through me, I succeed.

Jesus was not kidding when He said His Kingdom is not of this world. It is utterly antithetical to this world. Upside down. Inside out.

---

2. Hatmaker, Jen. *Interrupted: When Jesus Wrecks Your Comfortable Christianity.* Colorado Springs, CO: NavPress, 2014.

Bottom up. The first are last, and the last are first. He is a radical God who reigns over the craziest, most radical of kingdoms.

It's a Kingdom where the costs are great but the rewards are greater. A place where fear and sacrifice are real, yet it is these very factors that make the journey oh so worth it. God's Story is an epic tale of passion and adventure. It is an experience unlike any other. It's a journey where the Holy God of the Universe chooses to indwell us, gives us His mighty power, and partners with us to accomplish immeasurably more than all we could ever ask or imagine (Ephesians 3:20)! Why? So that we may have the richest experience of God's presence in our lives, completely filled and flooded with God Himself (Ephesians 3:20 AMP).

It's funny, for years I have known all these things in my head, but now I am beginning to know them in my heart. I am not becoming like God; He is coming alive in me. I am slowly dying, withering away, but He is coming alive. As John the Baptist once so prophetically said, "He must become greater; I must become less" (John 3:30).

Do Your thing, Jesus. Do Your thing.

Have Your way in us as we boldly step away from our prison cells and escape to an untamed, unchartered, mysterious, radical, and oh so set-apart life buried deep within the pages of Your Story.[+]

+ For discussion questions for this chapter, check out page 52 in the complimentary guide *Plan Your ESCAPE*. You can download it for FREE at HeatherRaeHutzel.com/PlanYourEscape

WANT MORE?

The book is finished, but that doesn't mean the journey is over.

If you want to dive deeper, then visit heatherraehutzel.com/signup to get a free digital copy of my Bestselling novel, *The Story of Life*. You can also hear about my soon-to-be-released series, *ANOINTED*, and how I recently pitched it as a movie to SONY.

ONE FINAL THING...

If you enjoyed this book, I would greatly appreciate it if you would leave a review. A review is the best way for you to express your thanks to an author, that and telling a friend about the book.

If you'd like to leave a review, please visit heatherraehutzel.com/reviewescape

Thank you for your support!

ABOUT THE AUTHOR

Home is Cincinnati where I live with my amazing husband and "do life" with an awesome community of Christ-followers. I'm an introvert by nature and an extrovert by necessity. You'll often find me writing (outside when the weather is nice). And when I'm not writing... I'm still outside! Spending time in my garden, taking photographs, tending bees with my husband (Yes, I said bees!), or playing frisbee with my best buddies, our dogs Westen and Finnley.

My journey of discovering what it truly means to live in God's radical story began shortly after publishing my Bestselling novel, *The Story of Life*. What that meant for me was quitting my job in the marketing research industry in order to pursue a God-given dream–a dream to unite and prepare this army called the Church for the return of her King.

My passion is inspiring and challenging the Church to abandon the status quo of watered-down, Americanized Christianity in order to pursue a radical, sold-out Kingdom life. I want others to experience the "MORE" God has for them!

To find out more, visit my website at heatherraehutzel.com

CPSIA information can be obtained
at www.ICGtesting.com
Printed in the USA
LVHW111514170119
604284LV00001B/138/P

9 780988 503649